A Book About

you

A Book About

you

Individuality and
Soul Awareness

David Green

MOSAICA PRESS

Mosaica Press, Inc.
© 2015 by Mosaica Press

Typeset by Esther Dishon

ISBN-10: 1937887502
ISBN-13: 978-1-937887-50-6

Published and distributed by:
Mosaica Press, Inc.
www.mosaicapress.com
info@mosaicapress.com

In loving memory
of my father

Herb Green, z"L
(Chaim Moshe ben Yitzhak)

He said little
yet did so much for so many.

His influence
as a creative and independent thinker
continues to inspire me
in all aspects of my life.

He is deeply loved and missed.

Contents

Acknowledgments

Wow, I can't believe this book is done. Complete... and I even like it. Trust me, it was not something I did on my own. There are many people whose direct and indirect help made this overwhelming project possible. Here we go:

I owe tremendous gratitude to my *Rebbi*, Rabbi Yaacov Haber, who not only enabled this book to be published but for years has been a source of inspiration and constant encouragement in all areas of my life.

Rabbi Doron Kornbluth and the editorial staff at Mosaica Press, for all your patience and professional guidance over the past two years.

Rabbi Eliezer Shore, for your deep insight and help with the writing of much of this book.

Eliyahu Berkowitz, for your encouragement and help in keeping my own personality alive throughout my writing.

Rabbi Dovid Slaven, Rabbi Eliezer Kwass and Jonathan Gabay for your feedback.

My amazing wife, Judy, whose love, caring and partnership shines through everything I do. My awesome kids and grandkids, who are always a great source of pride and joy.

I must thank my mother for being my Mom, "Bobo" for my kids and grandkids, literary critic, supporter of this project and great shmoozer over really good coffee.

And of course to God, for giving me a life full of talents and challenges that are all part of what is constantly shaping me to fulfill my real purpose in this world including the opportunity to share this important message with you.

Foreword

Rabbi Yaacov Haber

"Why was I created?" "What am I doing here?" "Who am I?" The most basic questions of life are indeed the most trying ones. Life is complicated.

Rabbi Eliyahu of Vilna or the Vilna Gaon (1720–1797) taught: "Every person must choose a different path on which to walk. There are no two minds, two faces or personalities that are the same. During the days of prophecy every person would visit the Prophet of his time. The Prophet would inform them, by accessing his prophecy, the path that is correct for them. He would stare into the depths of his visitor's soul, analyze it and discover the essence of the person's individual personality. After the cessation of prophecy there was still a lingering spirit which everyone possesses" (Gr"a, Proverbs 16:4).

Reb Tzaddok HaKohein (1823–1890), in a life altering essay, informs us that at some point in every person's life, God grants them a holy moment, or sort of prophecy. This is not a Messianic vision or a prediction of doomsday but rather a prophesy which presents a vision or a picture of himself or herself; not as he looks now but of how he would look as the greatest individual he can become.

In Kabbalistic language this form of prophecy is referred to as *Isarusa d'Leila* or *an awakening from above*. This vision is not a result of the toil of man but rather it is a gift from the Heavens, a clear job description, and a wake-up call from God.

Like every inspirational epiphany, *this awakening vision* must be closely followed by an *awakening from within* or in the language of the Zohar, an *Isarusa d'lsata*. In order to have a lasting affect, all things spiritual must be brought down to earth and internalized. One must strategize, plan and work to make their personal prophecy happen.

Sadly, most people do not take this second step. After having this dream, after experiencing this holy moment, most people push themselves back into a state of imagined reality and forget or try to forget what they have seen. They have thrown away a gift from God. God has just shown us what we can become, what to strive for, what is our raison d'être in this lifetime and we push it away.

The Talmud states that when the people of Israel left Egypt and stood before the split sea each and every Jew received a prophecy. "Even a simple person saw at the split sea what even the greatest of prophets, Ezekiel, couldn't see." In a matter of moments every Jewish man and woman were transformed from slaves to holy prophets.

Imagine the day, a million Yechezkel's and even more. What did they see? What did God tell all of these people? Where are their books of prophecy?

The answer is, their prophecies were not about the future and not about Messianic times. Their visions were about themselves. When the people of Israel crossed the sea it wasn't to get to the other side, it was to become *"a holy people and a nation of priests"*. Every Jew was shown an image of what he or she can become, why they were created, and what is their unique contribution to the world. As they left Egypt and crossed the split sea they became free to achieve greatness. Their individual prophecy became their charge, as it is ours, to work tirelessly to meet that goal and to come into our own. (Based on Rav Tzadok HaCohen; *Tzidkas Hatzadik*)

In other words, life is not entirely a guessing game. God gives us a hint and even a minor prophecy of what our life can become. As it is with all prophecies, what is presented to us is not necessarily the easy way or the path of least resistance. The prophecy presents a tailored fitness program that will allow us to realize why we were created. Once we know the goal, every decision and path we take becomes strategic in achieving our greatness. The RAMCHAL in his classic book *Mesilos Yeshorim* (Moshe Chaim Luzzatto 1707–1746) begins his book with the charge *"It is the basic obligation of every Jew to clarify and internalize the reality of his purpose in this world."*

One of the most moving events in the Torah occurred immediately before the death of the patriarch Jacob. Jacob gathered all his children around his death bed and directed them to listen carefully while he blessed them and told them what would happen to them at the end of days. The Hebrew word in the Torah that is usually translated as "happen" is peculiarly spelled with an aleph at the end. The word *"yekara"* spelled with an aleph actually translates as "will call". To translate correctly, Jacob summoned his children and said to them *"Gather as one, and I will tell you what will be calling to you at the end of days."*

Jacob taught his sons and all of Israel a fundamental principle. There will come a time in your life when you will hear a calling. When you hear it, it may seem unrealistic or naive. But when you hear it don't turn away. Grab it. It is yours to attain. If you turn around and go back to sleep it will slip through your fingers. A life is a terrible thing to waste.

The Purim miracle. The Jews in Persia are in serious trouble. A Hitler named Haman is on the loose. The King Achashverosh is inaccessible. Miracle of miracles, our very own beautiful Queen Esther is perfectly positioned in the royal court to approach Achashverosh to plead for the safety of her people, the Jewish people. Mordechei approaches Esther and charges her with the responsibility of saving her brethren. But Esther hesitates and wonders whether it is practical to approach the King of Persia. It was likely that she would be sentenced to death for gratuitously advising or correcting the king. Mordechei, seeing her fear, tells her, *"Esther! Who knows? Maybe it is for this very reason that you have become the queen."*

"Who knows!" Who doesn't know? It's obvious to all who read the book why Esther was so positioned to begin with. She was obviously meant to play a leading role in the miracle about to take place!. When God split the sea for the Jewish people, did any Jew say **"Maybe** it's for me to walk through? **Who knows**?!"

But Esther didn't know and neither was the great Mordechei so sure. What is more startling, however, is the rest of Mordechei's statement. *"And if you don't seize the opportunity at this time, the Jews will be saved by some other means, but you and your family will be lost".* In other words, 'Esther, do you want in?' Esther had a chance to stand up and be counted. It was her decision to make. She listened to Mordechei, she understood her own calling, she understood what she must do. She approached the king and saved the people of Israel.

The Talmud tells a story. Rabbi Tarphon was ill and his very important friends, Rabbi Akiva, Rabban Gamliel and others, came to visit. They met his mother at the door crying. She pleaded with the great men to "please pray for her son Tarphon-he is such a good son." She continued to tell them how once she was walking with her son Tarphon and her sandal slipped away. Tarphon immediately knelt before his mother, and put his hand under each of her feet as she walked so that she would not feel the pain of the stones and the twigs.

Rabbi Akiva upon hearing this story declared, "Tarphon has not even reached half of the obligation of a son to a mother!"

Such harsh insensitive words! What could be greater? What more could you do for your mother than walk backward before her on your knees with your hands under her bare feet?!

I heard a fascinating explanation for this from Rav J.B. Soloveitchik z"l. If you would have asked Rabbi Tarphon why he was created and what was his purpose in life, he would certainly have told you that he saw himself as one of the Baalei Mesorah-which he was. It was his job to soak in Torah from the previous generation, analyze it, and transmit it to the next generation, which he did. Certainly a worthy purpose. But when the great leaders heard of the exemplary way in which Tarphon treated his mother, they realized that his purpose was perhaps an even deeper one. He would be the paragon of ones obligation to respect his parents. His job was to set an example, and be a role model to the next generation. This was to be Rabbi Tarphon's special contribution.

Rabbi Akiva realized that perhaps Rabbi Tarphon had so excelled in his mission that God was ready to take him from this world. Rabbi Akiva's statement "Tarphon has not even reached half of the obligation a son has to a mother!" was actually a blessing. Since Rabbi Tarphon had not yet fulfilled his purpose, he could go on living! The purpose of his life had still not been achieved, his prophecy was not yet fulfilled.

During the High Holiday prayer service we add a sighing paragraph to our Amidah:

"Oh God! – before I was formed I was unworthy, and now that I have been formed, it is as if I had not been formed."

Rabbi Avrohom Yitzchok Kook (1865-1935) explained. Although our souls were already created at the very beginning of time they were not ready to be brought into this world. Our time had not yet come. For almost 6000 years our souls were in a holding pattern, waiting for their moment on stage. "Until I was formed I was unworthy!" Finally my time comes. After millennia I am pushed on stage – and I forgot my lines. "It is as if I was not created."

In our daily prayers we say: *"He is the Healer of the broken-hearted, and the One Who bandages their sorrows. He counts the number of the stars, to all of them He assigns names."* (Psalms 147) What is the connection between these verses?

Rabbi Shlomoh Freifeld (1925-1990) explained as follows: Many people are broken-hearted because they feel that their lives are insignificant. Every person needs to feel that he or she is

xvi   A Book About YOU

recognized, needed and appreciated. Even though they have light to contribute, they feel like the stars in the heavens. Each one is great, but there are so many, that most of them seemingly go unnoticed, and many are never even seen.

King David had a healing message for the brokenhearted and for all who feel ignored and insignificant: Each star counts; each star is noticed by God. Not only does each one count, each one has a name, assigned to it by God. Each star has a unique contribution to make.

David Green, in his insightful collection on what is perhaps the most important topic in life, helps us all realize our prophecy.

May we all be privileged to be awake for the call, to fulfill our task in this world, and to drink from the waters of Eden in this world and the next.

Rabbi Yaacov Haber

Rav, Kehillat Shivtei Yeshurun

Ramat Beit Shemesh, Israel

Introduction

Traveling Inwards

When I was only sixteen years young, for some reason my parents allowed me and a friend drive from Toronto to California to shop our songs around in the music business. For three months we stayed in "The Valley," the black ghetto of Watts with some amazing musicians we happened to meet, and then in a mansion in Beverly Hills. We traveled to places we had never seen before and met the most amusing personalities every step along the way, including some of my favorite musicians and producers. We befriended people living in the lowest of the lows and the highest of highs, in streets and palaces, and in the studios of Los Angeles. We got to experience an inside view into the lives of people who were regularly being arrested for suspicion of unlawful conduct, as well as some of the most successful TV and music producers of the time (some also criminals). It sounds like fun but it wasn't. It was so much more than that. It was awesome!

What about you? Are you also a traveler? What excites you? Where does your soul long to be? Do you dream of lush rain forests, broad savannas and ancient monuments or does your soul long for bustling cities? The desire to travel — to learn about new things, encounter different people, and expose yourself to wholly unique and challenging situations — can lead to the most enriching and mind-opening experiences that life can offer. Traveling opens the mind to new worlds and experiences, many of which stay with a person for the rest of his life.

But there is one destination that surprisingly few people take the time to truly discover. It is the most exotic, important place of all and the journey to get there is the most difficult you will ever take. It is that place deep inside your inner self — your soul. It is the essence of what makes you who you really are as a human being and as an individual. Your soul is a vast, pristine land whose beauty surpasses any place you can imagine on Earth. Getting to know that inner self is essential to enable you to build your relationship with God and to know why you were created and meant to achieve in this world. Without this awareness, we are lost in a confusing world telling us to be everything except that which will truly make us fulfilled. Yet, most people have not taken the journey to discover the most essential part of who they are.

I would like to welcome you on this journey to your soul where we will explore not only what your soul is but we will discover how yours is unique in its character and purpose in this world. As we embark inward to discover the world of your soul, try to tap into the exciting and explorative spirit of traveling.

In my more recent years as a musician, I wrote a series of songs all about this inner journey. Here is the chorus from the title song, "Journey to the Real You":

> *I'm going traveling across the world inside of me*
> *Climb some mountains, try to take in the scenery*
> *Find out what I'm missing out on*
> *Ways of life I've never seen*
> *I'm going traveling, traveling*
> *Journey to the real you*[1]

---

1.   From my song, "Journey to the Real You."

A Little Background

I grew up as an artist. My life was about writing music and being creative. I hung around with artists and followed the strict *halachos* (laws) of the religion of art. The rules of the game were that you must be authentic and unique, and most of all, you must be who you really are. Honestly, most of us were just faking being authentic, but please don't tell anyone.

When I started to become my true Jewish self, one of the things that really bothered me was what seemed to be the lack of personality and individuality in the religious world. So many people dressed the same and talked and walked to the same boring melody. I was not ready to abandon my true inner uniqueness for the sake of becoming a Jewish soldier dressed in uniform. As I started learning some of the deeper Torah sources, I saw how being a robot in my observance was the last thing God wanted of me. My unique qualities were supposed to blossom within the framework of a life of Torah and *mitzvos*. I discovered that true observance of God's will was not about becoming one of *them or*-blending into the crowd. I discovered that it was about becoming who I truly am and living the life that I am brought into this world to live. The sincere connection to Hashem is something that is so easy to let slide by the wayside, even while busy trying to do His will. Torah became the guide to enable me to live a unique, creative life, and discover myself as an individual and as an artist. Torah taught me how to really do what I had been faking in the world of music school.

Unfortunately, I still see a lot of unhappiness even in the religious community that could be overcome by giving ourselves a space to be who we really are. We need to serve Hashem in the unique way he created each of us to serve Him. How can we expect people to be happy if they are taught that they must wear a mask and take on someone else's identity, even if it is their rabbi or someone else who happens to be very holy? A true teacher should help you find yourself and how you can fulfill your role in serving God, not push you into a suit that simply wasn't tailored for you.

I hope our journey will help ignite that spark of individuality and sincere love of Hashem and a Torah way of life.

Three Friends

Our first stop on our journey is to meet three characters who will be joining us through much of our travels. In fact, I don't think they will seem like strangers to you at all.

You've met him. He's the type of person that seems more alive around people, lives in the moment, but is always late and unorganized. He enjoys a beautiful sunset or a pretty flower, loves music, is exceedingly generous with his time and possessions, but he is clueless when it comes to scheduling priorities effectively. Oh, and he loves to give really big hugs. I know this type of person. They come in all shapes and sizes. They are young and old, male and female, black and white. You find them in the strangest places. In fact, I am happily married to one of them.

How about the type of person who is well disciplined, usually on time, and organized? He pays attention to detail, is neatly dressed and keeps to a strict schedule. He tends to overlook emotional needs for the sake of practical responsibilities, and has good management skills. He is a very hard worker, perhaps even a workaholic. He tends to be the disciplinarian and is really bothered by injustice. Oh, and by the way, he absolutely hates really big hugs.

Okay, one more type. I am sure you know him.... He likes reading and deep thinking, and enjoys coming up with interesting ideas. He is blessed with a sense of balance in giving, never overextending himself or being stingy. He sets boundaries that are good for him and those around him. He hates hypocrisy and is somewhat cynical. He overlooks the superficial, external matters, never caring enough to tuck in his shirt, but never negligent enough to let it come entirely undone. He spends a lot of time on his own... even while in a crowd of people. Oh, and sorry to say, he might be perhaps a little on the egotistical side... but rightfully so. How would *you* feel if you were more intellectual than most of the world out there?

I am sure you can think of a few people that fit into each of the above descriptions. That is because our Sages teach us that the events describing our forefathers, Abraham, Isaac and Jacob, go well beyond describing the greatness of their lives and actions. They each represent one of three primary personalities reflecting God's attributes of *chessed*, *gevurah* and *tiferes*. They were each rooted in one of these *middos*, and so are we. Of course our forefathers, together with their wives, were able to express their main attributes without going overboard and losing balance. But for most of us, this balance is much harder to achieve. We see the patterns of negative traits but they come with the positive traits. We should all strive to have a healthy balance of all three attributes, but there are tremendous benefits to discovering the root personality of your soul. This will help determine where to concentrate your efforts in life, both by utilizing your natural strengths and by dealing with the likely weaknesses that come with your personality type when balance is not established.

Now take a few minutes to look at the descriptions again and rate which one describes you the most. This is not a theoretical question. Take a few moments and consider which one you really are.

Is it not so easy to identify? That's usually the case. Most people don't think about themselves in that way, and when they do, they get it wrong. That is because all three of these characters live inside of us but one of them is at the root of your soul's personality.

In the next few chapters, we will be traveling through a number of lessons and tools to help you discover the unique character of your soul. Once we have discovered your main personality type, we will then dig deeper down, layers below the surface, and uncover the essence of who you are and reveal what you were brought into this world to achieve. This book was written with the premise that only through the light of this inner awareness does one have a fighting chance of living a truly fulfilling life.

Okay, let's hear that again but with a bit more spice. The *Nesivos Shalom* said it best: "One who lacks this clarity of personal mission is like someone who wanders aimlessly in the streets, not knowing where he wants to go."[2]

This awareness will not only affect the way you view yourself, but it will have a profound effect on your relationship with others. For example, ask yourself which of the above personalities really bugs you the most. Do you find that you have a really hard time getting along with those who are always late or smother you with very big hugs? When I was in my twenties, I used to feel like there was something wrong with me for not giving massive mushy hugs to some of my hippier acquaintances — especially being a musician, since I was supposed to be the very expressive type. If I didn't take half the day to give them a hug from the sixties, I felt sure they were thinking, "What are you all uptight about?"

Are you uncomfortable around people who get uptight for the most ridiculous things, like keeping to a schedule or following all the rules to a T? What about those brainy types who are like walking computers without a heart? Do *they* get on your nerves?

There is a reason why you are more sensitive to certain types and not to others. It has to do with your personality as much as theirs. The more you understand why they act the way they do, the more you are likely to come to appreciate them for their differences and for the essential piece of the puzzle they contribute to the world... even if you are married to them.

---

2. *Nesivos Shalom*, vol. 1, "Awareness," chap. 5.

Overview of this Book

Who are you? Are you well acquainted with your own personality? What really sparks your sense of meaning and excitement in life? These are some of the questions we will be asking in Part One of this book. We will explore a number of questions to utilize the wisdom of Torah to help you identify the root of your soul's individual identity and purpose. This will be done by looking at some of the personalities described in the Torah and seeing how they are reflected within us. Once we have a good picture, we will advance to the big questions, such as how to choose a career and what your main purpose is in life.

Part Two explores the question: What are you? The answer is not, "I am a doctor," "I am a lawyer," or "I am a housewife." We need to explore and go much deeper than our external activities. We will look into what makes us human, the anatomy of the soul and its relationship to the body, and how that relates to shared principles of meaning and pleasure. Learning more about your soul will heighten your soul-awareness both intellectually and experientially in your daily life. This alone can be life transforming in a world that tries to convince us that bodily pleasures are all that matter. This spiritual awareness will also help you tune into the unique characteristics of your soul and life purpose. The more we are in touch with the needs of the soul in general, the more we can understand how our individual aspirations fit into the bigger picture of life.

In Part Three, we will discuss how to take what we have learned and make it real. We will tackle some of the challenges of making choices, prioritizing and channeling your natural strengths into what is most meaningful and practical.

Two Paths

There was a period of time when I was running a Jewish outreach program in Israel. I had so much going on that I couldn't take the time to listen to myself. I was a stranger in my own life. I was doing the wrong job for me. I was coordinating far too much; I found myself swamped in a sea of logistics — taking care of so many people and making sure that everything was done efficiently. That was the last job I should have been doing. But at the time, I didn't even consider playing any other piece of the puzzle. The problem was twofold. First, with so much buzzing through my mind, I couldn't even hear how disconnected I was from myself. Second, I did not appreciate the unique talents that God gave me to utilize productively in this world.

Throughout this book, we will be traveling down two parallel paths. One is focused on removing the distractions blocking our self-awareness. The noise of the world around us and the ongoing buzzing that takes place in our minds must be cleared away in order to hear the treasure that lies within. We will therefore be working to identify certain ideas, values and thinking patterns that interfere with our ability to tune in to what our souls are truly saying.

The other path is the positive process of defining what is inside of us. Learning what we can expect to find inside makes it much easier to identify what is buried within. So in a sense, while one path works to turn down the volume of the distractions of this world, the other lifts up the volume of the soul.

"Go to Yourself": The Original Jewish Journey

Taking a journey to your soul is not something I invented. Just look at the first words God said to the father of the Jewish nation: "*Lech lecha* — Go to yourself." The words, *lech lecha*, are commonly translated as "go for yourself." This means that God was promising Abraham personal greatness and good fortune if he left his home and moved on. However, an equally valid translation is "go to yourself." God was telling Abraham that he must discover himself first before he could fulfill his life's purpose.[3]

Taking this point a step deeper, God actually tells each and every one of us, "*Lech lecha* — Go to yourself," as a precondition to fulfilling our own individual mission in this world.[4] Today we don't have prophets to tell us what our Divine mission is in life, even if the guy in the robe on the corner claims he is one. You are required to be your own prophet. Although others such as our rabbis, family and friends can be of assistance, ultimately, we need to look inside ourselves and examine the way God created us, and see exactly who we are and what God brought us into the world to achieve. He created each of us in a unique way so that we can fulfill our unique piece in the "people puzzle" of this world.

Even though the greatest secrets of true happiness lie within, our tendency is to travel everywhere else in the world hoping to find it. After searching for meaning in the world of music, I finally realized that I had to go to Israel. I suddenly found myself in yeshiva with a group of like-minded men. They were inquisitive guys who had been everywhere in the world of thought and space before finally coming home to the hidden treasure inside of themselves. The first lesson I had on Torah text was on the words, "*Lech lecha.*"[5]

The Buried Treasure

Jacob Jakubowicz, a pious but poor Jew from the Kazimierz District of Kraków, Poland, dreamed that there was treasure hidden under the old bridge in Prague. Without delay, he made his way there. On arrival, it

---

3. *Kli Yakar* (Genesis 12:1).
4. *Sfas Emes* (Genesis 12:1).
5. Thank you, Tom Meyer.

turned out the bridge was guarded by a squad of soldiers and that digging was out of the question. Jacob told an officer about his dream, promising him half of the booty. The officer retorted, "Only fools like Polish Jews can possibly believe in dreams. For several nights now I have been dreaming that in the Jewish town of Kazimierz there is a hidden treasure in the oven of the home of the poor Jew, Jacob Jakubowicz. Do you think I am so stupid as to go all the way to Kraków and look for the house of this Jacob?" Jacob returned home immediately, took the oven apart, found the treasure and became rich. After this it was said: "There are some things which you can look for the world over, only to find them in your own home. Before you realize this, however, you very often have to go on a long journey and search far and wide." (See my song, "Long Journey" at www.realyouproject.com)

He also learned that you don't have to travel far to find your own, personal treasure; it lies deep within.

Today in Kazimierz, a shul still stands which was built using the money that Jacob found.

We must ask ourselves if such a valuable treasure is buried within, what is keeping us from looking inside to find the answers to our most meaningful questions in life?

The Challenge of "Going to Yourself"

Looking back on my life so far, I have to ask myself where I formulated my self-image. Since the moment I was born, I was profoundly affected by the people around me: my parents, family, teachers and friends. My gosh, the TV shows and movies I watched as a kid had so many assumptions portrayed about what was meaningful and, of course, cool. My favorite musicians taught me what to strive for not only in my art but also in my cultural expectations.

Besides the confusing values being conveyed, the overload of stimulation took control of my buzzing mind, making it almost impossible for me to sit still and listen to my own thoughts. It was always much easier to run to the next form of external entertainment. Now with the world speeding out of control, there is so much information constantly seeping into our minds, I find it an ongoing battle to really hear what my soul is trying to say.

There is an essential feeling that "getting away" is necessary to make changes. You need to go somewhere very different than your daily reality. Sometimes that requires a physical journey, but it always requires a mental shift. I used to love going skiing down the snow-covered mountains. Besides the heavenly feeling of being literally above the clouds as I drifted through the powder snow, I was in a very different world — one where I could see my life and see myself so much more clearly. That is the feeling I would like to capture as we continue our journey inwards. Let's try to get the same experience of clarity by trying to leave behind as much of our daily life and assumptions as we travel through the pages of this book. Like Abraham who was told, "Go to yourself," it all started with Go. Go away from the influences of your past in order to experience what is going on inside of you.

Taste the Tea

Okay, so sometimes you are with someone you love and as you communicate you really feel like you are there with them. Hopefully, they are there with you too. Then there are times when, for some reason, you just feel disconnected. Not because they turned you off about something, but simply because you are just a bit out of it that day. When this happens to me, I ask myself, *Why can't I live in the moment?* Perhaps I'm just too preoccupied with all the external responsibilities and concerns going on in my life. All the buzz and pressure to get things done is removing me from being with someone I really love. This struggle applies to our ability to experience ourselves as well.

Our preoccupied minds and hearts can easily numb us to the beauty and sensitivity to the world inside. My mother taught me this lesson many years ago.

I wasn't much older than eighteen. My life was accelerating way too fast, spinning out of control. I was living as if I was expecting to die by the time I hit the ripe old age of twenty. All I cared about was making it big in the music business and nothing was going to stop me. I was completely out of touch with everything else in my life. I had become numb to the world around me.

My mom, with her strong sense of perception and intuition, saw that I was in need of some good motherly guidance. But it wasn't going to be easy with someone who was far from being ready to listen. There is little value in rebuke to someone who is not ready to hear it. But she decided to give it a shot anyway.

"David, sit down," she said in her calm yet affirmative tone. *Sit down?* I thought to myself. *That alone was a major challenge for a restless soul like mine. What does she want to tell me this time?* But I saw that I was stuck. I had to sit down and wait this one out.

Then, instead of starting a lecture on how I should be spending more time on school or other priorities, she walked over to the other side of the kitchen and turned on the kettle. Next she took out a ceramic cup and some herbal tea. I liked ceramic, but *what was the point of herbal tea?* If I wanted a tasteless drink, I would prefer to drink water. Herbal tea had no flavor, and it cost more than regular tea. When the water was boiling hot, she poured some into the cup and then dipped the tea bag in a few times. By then I was completely confused. *At least try to squeeze out the little flavor that they say is hidden in this stuff. What are a few dips of the tea bag going to do even with regular tea?*

But to my mother, it was clearly part of her strategy to serve it like that. She placed it in front of me with the teaspoon still in the cup and said, "David, taste the tea." *Was that the point of this important mother to son meeting? Tasting some flavorless tea?* This wasn't love; it was some sort of psychological torture. It was hard enough finding time to eat yummy pizza, never mind boiling hot, tasteless tea. But what could I do? She had me cornered and I was not going to get out of this one.

The tea was far too hot to just start chugging it down the way I consumed everything else in my life. My impatient nerves were already frying from the injustice of having to sit this one out so long. Finally I took a teaspoon full, blew on it enough to cool it down for my first taste and sure enough I was right. There was nothing to taste. Well that's what it seemed like to me at that confused time in my life. But in reality, there was plenty of taste in the tea. There just wasn't anyone there to taste it. I had become completely desensitized to anything with less flavor than a Grammy award or a hit record.

In fact I was so hyperfocused on a vision of success for my future that my life in the present had become one of a walking dead man. No time for real life. No more taste buds for food, people and certainly not for the beautiful world that surrounded me all the time. But the biggest tragedy was that I couldn't hear the voice of the real David that was calling out from somewhere deep inside. How was I ever to become satisfied if I had no idea what I was looking for in my life, or the ability to experience it, even when I happened to stumble across it in the midst of my crazy life? Being out of touch was the perfect formula for unhappiness and my mother was able to spot it right away.

My mother had to stop me, slow me down and tune me back into life; the life around me and the inner life. Who knows how long I would have continued on this speeding train had she not stopped me. Ever since she said those words, Taste the tea, they have become a little alarm that goes off in my mind when I find myself moving too quickly or too intensely to experience the subtleties of life where the best flavors are found. Often the people we live with are the ones we least appreciate, and yet with a little effort to stop and "taste the tea" we can come to appreciate how blessed we are to be able to share our lives with them. With our

xxx   A Book About YOU

minds constantly being inundated with other people's visions, it requires a conscious effort to acquire the skill of living in real time. It takes a different way of looking at things. It takes patience to digest what we see, a chance to try it on and see if it really fits. But it's worth it, even for just a little peace of mind.

Dear river won't you slow down
Won't you grace me with a little show of my reflection?
Can't you see my current state of mind is far too
Blurred by self deception?

All I'm looking for is inner peace
But all I see is my scattered image looking back at me
When do you ever clear your waves?
To share your calm and blissful moments of clarity

Chorus
River, won't you share your peace of mind
Show me how to heal my troubled mind

Dear river flowing under me
When will you let me see below the surface waves of
    confusion?
When do you ever clear your waves
To share your calm and blissful moments of clarity?[6]

---

6.   Lyrics from my song, "Peace of Mind."

Part I

Who Are

YOU?

A World of Distinction

We all know that the importance of Jewish unity goes well beyond the feeling you get at a good *kumzitz*. Unity is one of the most important goals we can strive for, but it is so elusive. It doesn't come from just physically getting close. We need to put in effort. There are many beautiful analogies that emphasize the necessity for us to feel the pain of our brothers and sisters. On a metaphysical level, our unity achieves great spiritual heights, which opens the gates of tremendous blessing. On a day-to-day level, it can be as simple as giving a friendly smile or saying hello to the clerk at the supermarket. Those small gestures can open up enormous worlds. Even more so when we come together if the Jews are in trouble. But what if you don't agree with your neighbor? What if they think, act and talk differently? How am I supposed to have unity with that creep who lives down the block?

In fact, that is exactly where real unity is expressed—not when you are the same but when you are different. Just as a couple should love each other, building upon what each one brings into the relationship, so too, must we learn to love our neighbors for their differences.

So where must we start in creating such unity? The first person whose uniqueness you must appreciate is your own. It's only when each of us knows which piece of the puzzle we are meant to fill that the whole picture can be completed. If the violinist decides to pick up a trombone, the whole orchestra is in big trouble. Knowing who we really are as individuals is therefore essential to our unity as a nation.

"When I die and stand before God, He will not ask me why I was not Moshe Rabbeinu; rather He will ask me why I was not Zusha."[1]

> *A bicycle wheel has many spokes all branching out from the middle axle at different angles. They are connected by the outer wheel that unifies all of them. If one spoke is missing, the stability of the whole wheel is lost. So too, it is the essential contribution of our unique differences that will ultimately unify us in our service of God.*[2]

The Kabbalah describes how the world was created from oneness. God then took His original spark of creativity and divided it throughout the generations. Mankind started with Adam HaRishon and then expanded into millions of people with diverse personalities and contributions to the world. This is known as *Olam Perudah* (the world of distinction). Eventually, it is through our contributed efforts that unity will be expressed.

---

1. Rav Zusia of Anipoli.
2. R. Yaacov Haber, class on *Kedushas Shabbos*, Rav Tzadok.

Like a Brother

Welcome to the world of distinction
A world where I am I and you are you
Where everybody's got a point of view

Rise above the fear of contention
Listen to the beauty in diversity
Let everybody play their part from the inner melody
We're living in a symphony

Gonna make it through this stormy weather
I know there's something higher holding us together
One family, made to last forever
Just hold tight it'll be alright

Listening to the thunder and the lightning
Together with the rain and the blowing trees
See how the colors come together
In perfect harmony
We're living in a symphony

Gonna make it through this stormy weather
I know there's something higher holding us together
One family, made to last forever
Just hold tight it'll be alright.
I love you like a brother [3]

---

3. Lyrics to "Like a Brother" based on a class about the topic *Olam Perudah* given by R. Yaacov Haber.

↜Your Personal Torah

The Midrash says that an angel teaches us the whole Torah while we are in our mother's womb. This Torah taught to us goes beyond the written and oral law. It includes the "personal Torah" designed specifically for each and every one of us. There is a specific set of "*Toras chaim*" (instructions for living) that was given to you in order for you to know how to actualize your individual purpose in this world. They are instructions that were given to you and no one else. They have to do with your gifted strengths and weaknesses and what you are here to accomplish in your lifetime.

"It is not the individual who knows the Torah; rather it is the Torah inherent in the person that becomes his Torah."[4]

↜True Colors

There is nothing more fulfilling than to actualize this true divinely ordained inner purpose and mission. But in order to do so one must discover their true colors. Before any particular skills are developed, you must first find the deepest positive traits that you have been given as your own. This is the basis for everything you do. Only through guarding the qualities that are already yours can you become complete, because, in truth, the entire basis for a person's service comes from the qualities that exist in him naturally.[5]

So how do you find your true mission? If someone asks you to tell him what path he should take, your answer should be that he must pursue the path that his heart desires within the broad realm of Torah and *mitzvos*.[6]

Okay. I am listening to my heart. The problem is I don't hear much more than a pulse. To actually hear what is going on in one's

4. R. Menachem Mendel of Kotzk.

5. R. Yeruchom Levovitz, quoted in *Alei Shor*, vol. I, p. 146.

6. *HaEmek Davar*, *Bamidbar*, 15:41.

heart—to know what is sincere and what is just the sounds of outside influences—is not an easy task. That is why our journey to the soul is written with tools and insights to help make this an easier process.

⌒Love Yourself, Love Your Neighbor

The more you love yourself, the easier it is to love your neighbor. As we explore how to recognize individual personality traits, you will not only learn to love yourself better, but it will serve as a powerful tool to apply the principle of love your neighbor as yourself. Implicit in this statement is that the more you love yourself, the more you will love your neighbor. The reason for this is twofold. One reason is that the more you appreciate yourself, the more you believe in what you have to offer others. The second advantage is that the same system you will use to understand yourself better will enable you to see what makes other people think and act the way they do. You will start to appreciate how different people have been blessed with individual attributes that are meant to help and challenge them in fulfilling their purpose.

As we will see, every strength comes with a vulnerability to a related negative trait. If someone behaves in a way that really bothers you, it is often related to a positive quality they have. Understanding how these positive and negative attributes overlap makes it much easier to be tolerant of their weaknesses. It also helps people overcome their tendencies toward jealousy since other people are viewed as having very different demands and opportunities that should not be compared with your own.

While in college in Bloomington, Indiana, I rented a room in a house off-campus with other students. Sometimes, I found myself with others whose rooms were as messy as mine. Other times, I found myself stuck with people who were extremely uptight about anything you could imagine. The most obvious symptom of their disease was that they were the biggest clean freaks brought down to this planet. The obsession with neatness drove me crazy.

Thinking back now, I realize that what I perceived to be a problem of being uptight was just the flip side of being very precise and organized, which is a great quality. It was a quality that I desperately needed in order to become a better-rounded person. It's scary to think of all the years of my life I must have spent looking for things.

Now when I meet people who "rub me the wrong way" rather than judging them for their seemingly negative quality, I try to ask myself what quality it is that they have that I should be improving upon.

∼ Paradigms of the Soul, Fathers of the Nation

As mentioned in the introduction, when we first look within ourselves in an attempt to identify our unique personality traits, we find three primary attributes, *chessed*, *gevurah* and *tiferes*. In Part Two of this book, we will explore some of the kabbalistic meaning of these attributes and how they relate to the makeup of a human being and the world as a whole. We will first explore how these attributes manifest themselves in the primary personality types. While every person must try to create a healthy dose of all three in order to be stable, we see that people embody one trait more than the others. There are many sources in the Torah that refer to this set of three attributes. If you examine them closely you will find that they can always be traced back and rooted to these original three and the Patriarchs that embody them. For example, *Ethics of the Fathers* says: "The world stands on three things—Torah, *avodah* and *chessed*." Corresponding to Torah is *tiferes*, to *avodah* is *gevurah*, and *chessed* remains *chessed*. Just as the world stands on all three, so does every individual, being a microcosm of the world. Yet our primary attribute must still be developed with great effort.

> One who feels a special pull toward a specific area of good deeds, whether it be Torah study, prayer or acts of kindness for others, he must realize that this is his connection to the Tree of

*Life [i.e., Torah], and through that area he is rooted in holiness.
It is through this point that he can build himself up and become
elevated [in all areas], if he takes care to invest great effort in
it constantly, never abandoning it.*"[7]

~ When Insecurities Get in the Way

It is important to point out that in many cases people have
insecurities that make it difficult for them to comfortably express
their primary attribute. For example, I have met people who are
Chessed personalities. But even though there is nothing more they
want than to be able to connect with people, they are shy due to
low self-esteem or fear of rejection. But since their main driving
force is the desire to connect, we can see that they are, nonethe-
less, *Chessed* personalities. It is important when exploring your
root personality type to ask yourself what it is you would enjoy
most, even if you find it difficult to do.

Once you really get to really know yourself, the easier it will be
to love yourself. You will start to feel a deeper connection with the
real person inside. This is a very healthy form of unconditional self-
love, much like the deep love parents have for their children. So really
getting to know yourself makes your insecurities fade away.

In Part Two, as we explore the spark of divinity within every
one of us, we will directly address the challenge of building your
self-esteem.

~ Transform Your Marriage

If you are married, do you really appreciate your spouse? Do
they appreciate you? Do you feel it? Does the appreciation sink
in, arrive at your heart? Learning to love yourself and appreciate the other's strengths and weaknesses is a powerful means

---

7. R. Abraham Pam, *Atarah laMelech*, p. 176.

to transform your marriage. As we learn to identify what makes people click, it becomes much easier to appreciate the essential piece of the puzzle that your spouse is providing and how to bring those qualities out in them. It will also become easier to face the frustrations that arise from not understanding why they don't see things the way you do. It is the differences between the two of you that are what make the deeper love grow. Through understanding those differences, the potential of your relationship starts to fit together with the appreciation of how you truly complement each other. Many marriages suffer when the partners lose touch with what they each offer the relationship.

> *Come take a look in my eyes and see what I see*
> *I'm only searching to find the one in front of me*
> *I'm looking deep in your eyes and see what I see*
> *The beautiful world you deny is ready to be free.*
>
> *You need to believe me that*
> *I love your true colors*
> *I want no other but the real you*
> *I love your true colors*
> *You need to discover the inner beauty that you never*
>   *knew*[8]

ᐦ Personality and Jewish Learning

Being aware of your personality plays a powerful role in becoming more motivated and deciding which aspects of Torah learning to focus on. By allocating enough of your Torah study time to the topics that inspire your specific personality type, you will find yourself

---

8. From my song, "Real You" (True Colors).

enjoying it much more. This will serve as an inspiration to appreciate the beauty in other areas of study as well. *Chessed* personalities enjoy learning more about topics of spirituality, philosophy of prayer, *Ethics of the Fathers*, character refinement and, of course, Kabbalah. *Gevurah* personalities prefer halachah, Mishnah, and Gemara, as long as there is enough of a practical topic being discussed. If it is too esoteric, it will not keep them sincerely interested. The *Tiferes* personality tends to enjoy in depth Talmud, deep philosophy and a moderate dose of Kabbalah. Both the *Chessed* and *Tiferes* personalities are less naturally inclined toward practical halachah.

This is very important for Jewish educators to consider. Identifying the personalities of your students will enable you to design your teaching around what naturally inspires them and to help them appreciate more aspects of Torah learning. During my years of teaching in outreach programs, the questions asked, the way students dressed and their general mannerisms were all hints as to what to focus on as a starting point for our learning. Those that dressed more bohemian would use their initial question as a lead into talking about something spiritual or about a relationship with someone. The neatnicks holding notebooks often started with questions about a detail they may not have understood clearly but behind that was a fear that what they were learning was going to disrupt their already established life plans. Therefore, when meeting one-on-one, I would always try to get a snapshot of their personality in order to help me connect to the real person and the underlying issue behind the question being asked.

Not only is it critical for everyone to find their place within learning but we all have to find our place within the broader framework of Torah observance.

"A person can live a life of Torah and *mitzvos* and still not have begun to fulfill their individual purpose in this world."[9]

---

9. Arizal (quoted in *Nesivos Shalom*).

Journal

At the end of a number of sections you will find some "journal questions" designed to help make the ideas more lasting. Take some time to think and write down your answers. Let's start with a few questions based on what we have discussed so far.

1. How do you think you will benefit from getting to know yourself on a deeper level?

2. How would knowing yourself better affect your relationship with others?

3. How would knowing yourself better affect your relationship with yourself?

4. How would knowing yourself better affect your relationship with God?

5. Do you feel prepared to get to know yourself better?

6. What do you feel your biggest challenge is in knowing yourself better?

The *Chessed* Personality

I'd like to introduce you to someone you are bound to like. After all, most people just love him.

- *Chessed personality, please say hello to all my friends reading this book.*

- *Hey guys, it's really a pleasure to meet all of you. I hope to get a chance to talk and chill together with every one of you.*

Our friend is a people person to the core. Let me tell you about the last time I saw him.

I was considering ordering a second cup of coffee, but decided not to. If I drank a second cup now, what would I do when Abe finally showed up? Order a third cup? Just then, the door to the café flew open and in whisked Abe like a runaway spring breeze popping in for a cup of tea. He was the only person I knew who wore his Birkenstock sandals in the winter, but always had a long knit scarf around his neck. He waved at a person sitting in the back before bustling over to my table. Before I could say a word, I was smothered with a scarf and dragged out of my chair for a big bear hug that drew stares.

"Hey, brother! Am I late?"

"Well, actually..."

"Oh, I am so sorry. Didn't we say we would meet at three-fifteen?"

"Actually, we said three."

"Are you sure? I think I wrote it down." He began to dig through his bag, looking for a tattered date book I had occasionally seen him write appointments in.

"I'll get you a cup of herbal tea to make up for it." He signaled for the waiter and ordered two cups. I was about to call the waiter over to change my order to a double espresso when I sighed and resigned myself to my taste-free fate.

"I was sure I was going to get here on time. I left my house five minutes early but the bus was late and there was a woman on the bus that started talking to me and made me want to cry. Miriam is eighty years old and has no one. She needed to move some chairs up to her third-floor apartment. After that, she wanted me to stay for tea, but I knew you were waiting."

The next half-hour was taken up with an in-depth recital of a Kabbalah class he had attended in the morning. I looked at my watch and realized that I was already late for my next appointment. I had a doctor's appointment for a checkup. Abe saw me look at my watch and took it as a hint.

"I am so sorry that I am taking up too much of your time. It's on me, friend." He pulled out his wallet. He opened it, and his face turned red.

"I'm sorry. I forgot that I gave my last twenty dollars to a poor man I met on the way here that hadn't eaten in three days. I couldn't say no."

After paying, I got up to leave but Abe stopped me. "I was just on my way to the park. On the way in, I noticed that the leaves were just changing colors and I wanted to take some pictures. I know you are already late, but I can't imagine anything more wonderful than having a few photos of you in the park. Can you spare me the time?"

I pulled out my credit card and paid. I was about to explain about my next appointment, when I remembered how good my time with Abe always made me feel. I took a deep breath and dialed my phone. I was pleasantly surprised when the receptionist told me that the doctor was running behind in his appointments and I would be seeing him half-an-hour later. I figured time spent with Abe was the best medicine anyway.

In order to understand what Abe is really about, let's look into the roots of the *Chessed* personality.

It all started with Abraham, the first Jew and father of the Jewish nation. Keep in mind that we want to look at the roots of his personality in order to help us identify the same basic drives within ourselves. Through both his hard work and natural proclivity, Abraham became the personification of the trait of *chessed*, which means kindness, love and care for our fellow individuals. Most of the stories told in the Torah about Abraham and his wife Sara revolve around their totally selfless giving to others, both physically and spiritually, such as their readiness to have guests or Abraham's prayers for the wicked of Sodom. Abraham was able to love everyone, including the wicked, because he saw their potential for good. Rather than judging them by their external actions alone, he saw their inner spiritual beauty. He knew that each individual is created in the image of God, and thus was able to honor them. Abraham was the personification of the primary attribute of *chessed*. It is through him that we can begin to understand the *Chessed* personality.

Abraham's great outpouring of love made him a blessing to the people of his time, and implanted this desire to help others in the hearts of his descendants. The Torah states about Abraham: "You will be a blessing."[10] One aspect of this was that anyone who came in contact with Abraham, interacted with him or merely saw him, would be blessed, because Abraham himself had become a blessing. Indeed, a true person of *chessed* feels for others, and gives to them with his entire heart. When he sees another person suffering, the *Chessed* personality relates to him in the spirit of

---

10. Genesis 12:2.

the verse: "I am with him in his trouble."[11] And when his friend experiences joy, he stands beside him as a partner. The *Chessed* personality influences all who enter his sphere. He gives everyone his attention, because he loves every person as himself. An aura of love and fraternity accompanies him, as though his entire being is given over to assist the other. The *Chessed* personality embodies the unique nature of *chessed*, which is expansiveness (*hispashtus*). Thus, *chessed* and love emanate and extend from him, reaching both near and far. By contrast, the person who lacks *chessed* is, by nature, contracted and limited. Whatever capacity he has to love, he contains narrowly within, and applies it only to himself and his immediate family.

~ Are You a *Chessed* Personality?

In today's world of iPhones, YouTube and Facebook, all the attention seems to be directed inward upon the individual—it is all about me, me and more me. Yet, despite this predilection of society (some would call it an illness), one can still identify *Chessed* personalities. For example, since the emphasis of the *Chessed* personality is between one person and the next, we can assume that the soul of someone who is very much a people person is rooted in *chessed*, and is particularly connected to the forefather Abraham. These people feel a natural connection to others, which leads them to socialize more. And when someone is suffering, it pains him or her as well. Not only do they empathize with people in pain—even with those they do not know—they invest much time and effort in reaching out to others to help them. This is not motivated merely by the desire to do the right thing, but out of a genuine emotional caring for others that drives them to want to help.

---

11. Psalms 91:15.

My wife, Judy, and I were on a flight to Israel. We sat on each side of an aisle. On Judy's other side was a girl that she had never met before. After about ten minutes she turned to me and said this is my new friend, Shauna. She meant it. Of course by the time the flight was over, they graduated to become sisters. My wife has thousands of sisters who she met over the years, from the clerks at the supermarkets, poor people who have come to our door, people she met who were sitting at a nearby table at a restaurant and from numerous other places where you would never expect to make a friend. This is an important part of who she is—a *Chessed* personality through and through.

The *Chessed* personality's sincere care for their fellow man is part of a God-woven tapestry of natural qualities at the root of their soul which they were blessed with in order fulfill their mission in this world. The same gifted virtues are not limited to relating to others. There are many other ways that the *Chessed* personality utilizes these skills in other areas of life. It is also helpful for us to find more clues to identify a *Chessed* personality outside of the framework of an obvious act of love and caring. Let's look at some examples.

❧ Openness

To express love for someone else demands a sensitivity and awareness of what the other person is feeling. One must be able to set aside their own preconceptions of the other person's needs and wants, and truly become receptive to what is going on inside of them. This is one of the strengths of the *Chessed* personality. This sensitivity and openness also manifests itself in the *Chessed* personality's ability to feel inspired by the beauty and magnificence of the world around them, usually accompanied by a general sense of artistic and aesthetic appreciation. A similar openness and trust is often displayed in their penchant for health food, approaches to alternative healing, such as holistic medicine, meditation and other practices, which the other personality types tend to be more skeptical about.

This is why you must be very careful not to give your credit card to a *Chessed* personality. To understand, imagine life from their perspective. You meet someone trying to sell you a new kind of juice-making machine, herbal formula or anything else you never knew would enhance your already beautiful life. The first thing you notice is that the person selling the product seems to have such a special heart, really a beautiful soul. This is where your credit card starts to become at risk. But it gets much more dangerous. Watch what happens next.

Continuing from the eyes of our *Chessed* personality, you see them demonstrate how it works and they quote some people whose lives were transformed because of this great new contribution to mankind. It's okay that few people are aware of this product. You, as an open-minded persona, are used to considering all kinds of things that the stubborn world has yet to catch onto. Even though some people would get turned off by the aggressive sales job, you just see the beautiful soul trying to help you see the light. Even if you notice their obnoxious sales techniques, that too is okay since they are just trying to make a living and you would love to help them. Especially if they seem in any way needy, for at that point the product isn't even important. All that matters is that you are able to help them, even if you can't afford it. This explains the list of purchases on your Visa statement that don't seem to make any sense.

We will have more fun seeing how this quality goes overboard, but our goal now is to see that behind these bursts of spending is a beautiful quality of open-mindedness that helps the *Chessed* personality consider spiritual opportunities with the same willingness to participate.

⌒ Living in the Moment

In order for the *Chessed* personality to express love and empathy of others, they need to put aside everything else in the world for the time that they are devoting their full attention to the person in need. The ability to live in the present moment is a critical part of the package they are blessed with to enable them to naturally fulfill their true purpose. While some people's minds and hearts are already onto the next task on their list before they have even finished the present job, the *Chessed* personality is in one place at one time. Even when alone, his or her heart is fully dedicated to experiencing the most of whatever is in front of them at that particular moment. They can truly "taste the tea"—even herbal tea.

Living in the moment creates an excellent mindset for prayer or meditation with great intention. It is natural for this personality to get totally into it... for real. To the outsider it looks like they are faking it, but that Carlebach follower with the flowy clothes and colorful kippah is likely for real.

⌒ Social Causes

For the *Chessed* personality, the inclination to care for others finds expression in ways beyond merely showing kindness toward the individuals who happen to be in their life at the time. When a *Chessed* personality hears of people suffering on the other side of the world, their inner voice of empathy and love is ignited. It may result in their purchasing a plane ticket to actually travel there in order to help, or simply in giving charity for the sake of those unfortunate individuals. One of the surest ways of identifying a *Chessed* person is by how hard it is for them *not* to offer to help people in need.

～ People People

For a *Chessed* person, loving other people also means enjoying being around other people. This is not necessarily true
for everyone. A person may help others out of a sense of moral
responsibility, but not particularly enjoy being involved in other
people's lives. For the *Chessed* personality, however, being around
others is a source of inspiration in itself. They thrive on connecting to others even when there are no individuals who require their
help. They are "people people" by nature, which is expressed in the
warm and outgoing approach they show to everyone they meet,
from their good friends to the stranger they chat with on an eleva-
tor ride.

～ *Chessed* Overboard

The above are wonderful traits, all of which suggest openness and a proclivity to flow beyond boundaries. However, it is a
spiritual principle that even the noblest personality trait, if left
unrefined, can actually become destructive. Unrestricted *chessed*,
without the balancing influence of *gevurah* and *tiferes*, runs the
risk of degenerating into chaos, instability and irresponsibility.
When that happens, a *Chessed* personality can be identified by
the uniquely negative traits that they manifest. Identifying these
negative patterns is useful for two reasons:

1. To better help you know yourself. If you are a *Chessed* person,
   you may need to work on the following areas.

2. Even if you are not a *Chessed* person, you may well have to
   deal with unbalanced *Chessed* people in the course of your
   day, only to find their behavior mysterious and upsetting.
   By understanding that these negative traits are often major
   challenges of *Chessed* personalities, it makes it much easier
   to deal with them and accept them. In addition, your personal strengths, which may be expressions of a different per-

sonality type, can provide them with the balance they need to maximize their potential. They too may offer you a healthy dose of *chessed*, which will create a balance in your own life, and stretch you more in the direction of emotional sensitivity and love for others.

～ Being Too Open

Some people are "so open-minded that their brains are falling out," as the saying goes. It is a beautiful quality to be willing to explore new ideas and opinions, but one must do so with both feet firmly on the ground. That is, with a strong sense of intellectual honesty, and with a pragmatic view of how to actualize the idea being proposed.

The *Chessed* personality naturally lacks these two traits. They want to invest their energies in every new and exciting plan. However, without these elements of objectivity and practicality, they are at risk of being swept up in deceptive sales tactics, misleading "spiritual" practices and untrustworthy mentors who may have impure motives. If nothing else, the *Chessed* personality may simply waste their time on secondary endeavors, rather than investing their time and energy into things that really count for them in their lives.

For example, there's a new natural diet being recommended by the charismatic inventor—*but don't worry, he's not biased*. The diet will boost your serotonin, energy and peace of mind, as long as you take Chinese herbs and work out regularly as well. It's a holistic approach to solve all your physical and emotional problems.

But how do you know the workout and herbs are not making you feel better? Perhaps the diet has nothing to do with it. I know I sound skeptical but that's because I'm not an extreme *Chessed* personality. Of course, I wouldn't write it off completely, but before paying with my time and money, I would do some serious research to make sure it's not another scam.

When the *Chessed* personality starts to go overboard, he is the perfect target for such scams. A little critical thinking can save a lot of trouble. It's worth it.

～ **Always Late**

This is a classic sign of our good friend Mr. or Mrs. *Chessed*. While living in the moment allows the *Chessed* personality to fully experience the world and other people, it also makes them vulnerable to repeated lateness, and the problem of losing track of everything else in life that depends on time. Maintaining a schedule is a tremendous challenge for this type of person, so that even when committed to meeting someone somewhere, they are inevitably late. This is one of the most noticeable flaws of the *Chessed* personality.

They will call a friend who they love so very much (of course) and make up to meet at a coffee shop at eight o'clock. What time will they show up? Eight-twenty, if their friend is lucky. More realistically, closer to nine. How can they claim to love and care about their friend, if they are ready to make him wait an hour at the coffee shop?

But, of course, that is precisely the connection. Love is an expansive trait that knows no boundaries. It is precisely because they are inclined to love that they also struggle with keeping schedules. For someone who lives in the moment, there is little sense of when to leave the house and how long it may take to get somewhere. Often, they will leave their home at the very time they agreed to meet. The fact that it takes time to get there was not figured into their plans until they were well on their way. And even when they realize that they are late, they must still face numerous challenges along the way: friends they have not seen for a few days, telephone calls that must be answered (and woe to you if the other person on the line is also a *Chessed* personality), even a stray kitten that needs some milk. After all, if the *Chessed* person doesn't stop to care for them, who will? Such unrestrained behavior can easily add lengthy delays to the arrival time of our well-meaning friend.

⤿ Social Causes vs. Family Demands

The deep pleasure the *Chessed* personality finds in helping others and giving to the larger community also puts them at risk of forgetting those closest to them who rightfully deserve their support and attention. While they may love their family and close friends deeply, the responsibilities of day-to-day life are burdensome when compared to the exuberating feeling of helping many people with their problems. As a result, the very people who once felt the *Chessed* person's love pouring down upon them at an early stage of their relationship may now feel ignored, when their benefactor seeks to express himself by engaging in a larger degree of *chessed*. Unfortunately, when you see someone completely immersed in doing *chessed* for their community, it is often at the expense of others. Thus, the Chessed personality must know how to prioritize when to give, how much to give and to whom to give.

⤿ All You Need Is Love—Well, Not Really

The most dangerous distortion of *chessed* is when the boundaries are blurred in the most cherished relationships. For example, marriage is not just about how much love the couple share with each other. The depth and holiness of a marriage is created by the exclusivity of the couple's commitment to one another. These are the boundaries that are essential to making the love of a marriage as beautiful as it can be. Yet this commitment can be difficult for someone who is used to showing their love for everyone. Without proper limitations (the trait of *gevurah*), the stability of the *Chessed* personality's marriage can be seriously threatened.

Journal

1. Which of the positive qualities of the *Chessed* personality do you find within yourself?

2. List the *chessed* qualities and rate how strongly they motivate your actions, on a scale of one to ten.

3. Which of the weaknesses of the *Chessed* personality do you find within yourself?

4. Do you think you are a *Chessed* personality?

5. If so, why?

6. If not, why not?

The *Gevurah* Personality

I was on my way to the café once again. Ike had sent me an instant message this morning reminding me of our appointment. I was going to be a few minutes early, so I was surprised when I walked into the shop and saw Ike sitting at a table near the door. He was talking into his Blackberry and writing in a small notebook. I sat across from him and waited for him to finish.

"Okay, I understand. Of course this is serious. She needs help. Have her come into the office and fill out the proper form, listing all of the children and all of her expenses. That way, we will know exactly how much to give her. Also, make sure she fills out a form so that we can help her find a job."

Ike stood up and shook my hand, his hand firm and strong, two shakes and a quick release.

His hand went up to unconsciously smooth out his tie after he sat down. "That's what I like about you—always on time."

I smiled. "I thought it was my winning personality and gentle soul."

He nodded. "Well, of course, but it's so important to be on time. After our lunch, I have to run back to the office to meet with the committee that distributes charity to single mothers. We have a new woman in the community and her son's bar mitzvah is in two weeks. We have to organize the catering."

The waiter brought him a salad and I reconsidered ordering a hot chocolate brownie. I ordered an herbal tea and one of their low-cal desserts. It only tasted a little bit like cardboard but I convinced myself that I felt better after eating it. Ike told me about a class he was teaching in daily halachah. He was up to the section about *tzitzis* and how long the fringes had to be. I was fascinated, having no idea there were so many conflicting opinions. I always learn so much from my meetings with Ike that I get disappointed when he looks at his watch and nods, signaling the end of our time together. It is a bit of a comfort that before he leaves, he always takes a few moments to schedule in another get-together.

Directly opposite the trait of *chessed* is that of *gevurah*, which means "strength" and "fortitude." If the trait of *chessed* is to give and flow out without boundaries or discrimination, then the trait of *gevurah* is to set limits and boundaries, exercise control and discipline the inclination to boundless giving. On an emotional level, *gevurah* is associated with fear, as opposed to *chessed*, which is love. Fear causes you to withdraw and restrict yourself. However, the ultimate type of fear is fear of God, which leads to the ultimate type of limitation, which is self-restriction, as the Mishnah states, "Who is strong? One who can conquer his evil inclination."[12] That is, true strength is not measured in the ability to overcome someone else, but to restrain oneself from impulsive and destructive behavior. *Gevurah* is what sets limits to *chessed*, so that it does not express itself in inappropriate ways. On a societal level, *gevurah* is associated with laws and judgment. An altruistic society is a *chessed* society. However, if personal boundaries are not to be transgressed, society must also have laws and judgments to provide order and structure to communal life.

The attribute of *gevurah* was personified by Isaac, Abraham's son. It isn't that Isaac was physically strong, but that he had the utmost self-control and was able to conquer his evil inclination and rule over his animal soul. A person needs tremendous

---

12. *Ethics of the Fathers* 4:1.

discipline, obedience and determination to achieve his higher goals in life. Several biblical stories about Isaac reveal his ability to restrain himself in the face of fears and desires; the most obvious being his willingness to let himself be bound upon the altar—by his father—and offered as a sacrifice.

⮑ Are You a *Gevurah* Personality?

The *Gevurah* personality is recognizable by its high degree of discipline and self-control. Just as the *Chessed* personality is blessed with its variety of means for expressing their natural loving-kindness, so too, the *Gevurah* personality expresses itself in numerous, related forms. We will examine some of the natural attributes that are required to express *gevurah* and see how they manifest in other areas of life independently. If you identify strongly with these expressions, you are likely discovering the root of your soul's *Gevurah* personality.

⮑ The Demand for Justice

Unlike the *Chessed* personality, who identifies with the attribute of mercy, the *Gevurah* personality is driven by a demand for justice. They strongly affirm the belief that people are far better off if they work for what they receive, rather than get it as a free gift. If something hasn't been worked for, it seems cheap to them. Why should someone get something they don't deserve? That is breaking the rules of justice, and cheating the system. Justice must always prevail.

The *Gevurah* personality is therefore naturally attuned to the system of reward and punishment. While other personalities may run away from the idea of our actions having direct consequences, the *Gevurah* personality welcomes this idea, like a parent who recognizes the need to create consequences for his child who runs in the street. Justice can also be seen in the *Gevurah* personality's careful management of their money and other possessions. Damages to their own or other people's property is taken very seriously, for that is the "right" thing to care about, and actions are quickly taken to compensate whoever has incurred a loss.

~ Drive and Assurance

Gevurah personalities exude a sense of strength and self-confidence. They are often the leaders of groups and offices, and have the confidence and inner strength to stand up to demanding challenges. To a *Gevurah* personality, self-doubt is highly destructive, for they carry with them an inner conviction that if they work at something, it will pay off. Getting out of bed early in the morning, even when exhausted, is a *gevurah*-based gift. While other personality types will push the snooze button as many times as possible, the *Gevurah* type will get up, get dressed and start their day moving as quickly as possible. They are the first ones at the gym at five a.m. and the first ones at the office door at nine. The breadth and expansive space and time that the *Chessed* personality needs to feel comfortable and express itself in, to the *Gevurah* personality, is an expression of laziness and almost a sin. To the *Gevurah* type, giving up on a project before the end is almost unheard of.

This quality contributes to the *Gevurah* personality being great at sports and other types of physical labor. Early morning practices, repeated exercises, the drive to win and a belief in their ability to fight right to the end of any challenge makes the *Gevurah* personality a great person to have on your team.

~ Organized or Else

Being so goal-oriented, the *Gevurah* personality has a natural gift to work within the realm of what is practical (as opposed to the dreamy *Chessed* type). It is therefore part of their personality to be organized, and any form of disorderliness is perceived as an impediment to their goals. Thus, by nature, the *Gevurah* personality—like a well-trained soldier—is committed to following a plan with precision. Even unexpected emergencies are well-prepared for. Fire extinguishers, smoke alarms, emergency numbers on the fridge are among numerous precautions taken to keep all emergencies under control.

⤳ Always on Time

Similarly, the *Gevurah* personality regards time as an integral part of reality, and its rapid passing cannot simply be ignored. If a target moves off course, then something else must be sacrificed to realign oneself with it. That is why if you have plans to meet a *Gevurah* personality at eight p.m., you had better be there on time. Don't forget, your *Gevurah* friend will probably have already been there at least ten minutes early, having taken into account all the possible delays that may have occurred along the way. Nor do they mind arriving early, since it gives them a chance to make some important calls and review their schedule for the rest of the week. But don't dare be late!

⤳ Willingness to Accept Authority and Structure

While many people struggle with authority and structure because they feel that it restricts their creative or intellectual freedom, the *Gevurah* personality is more concerned about doing what is ultimately right than about expressing himself. He welcomes the leadership of others, if it helps him achieve that goal, however, this only works when the authority is trusted for their good strategic judgment. Otherwise it could be very frustrating for the *Gevurah* personality, if he is being asked to work unproductively.

✑ Formality

Consistent with their love of structure, discipline and organization, *Gevurah* personalities tend toward formality, orderliness and cleanliness. *Gevurah* personalities can be recognized by their clothing: their starched and pressed shirts neatly tucked in, free of all stains. A briefcase or laptop case is also a natural fit for our productive friend. Their home and office space is kept neat and clean. All of this makes them feel comfortable and in a positive and productive frame of mind.

✑ *Gevurah* Overboard

Just as the *Chessed* personality can show traits of imbalance when not complemented with a healthy dose of limitation, so can the *Gevurah* personality become imbalanced when not complemented by its fair share of *chessed*. Many people waste their lives in the pursuit of useless goals. Their strong drive to work actually obscures the whole purpose of their mission. A *Gevurah* personality can easily be busy from morning to night, though secretly, they are fleeing from living out their real goal and purpose in this world. Do you find yourself too busy to think about the bigger picture of life and its deeper meaning? Are you missing out on a deeper dimension of life for the sake of achieving something that has only a surface-level value? Do you feel that you lack too many of the attributes of the *Chessed* personality, discussed above?

Let's see some common examples of what can happen when someone lives with an imbalance of too much *gevurah*. This is meant not only as a warning to such people, but as a helpful tool to identify the *Gevurah* personality. It should provide us with the tools for tolerantly accepting people who are different from ourselves, by understanding that these are the weaknesses that most often come with the package of the good qualities.

ᕫ **Workaholism**

Have you ever wondered why workaholics work so hard to achieve? The *Gevurah* personality is extremely vulnerable to this tendency because they can so easily justify their actions through *gevurah*'s positive qualities. They feel energized when they are the most busy, and alive when they are filled with a sense of productivity. Unfortunately, the need for this feeling can become irrational, to the point where they become driven more by the need to stay active than to achieve the actual task at hand. As a result many important aspects of life that are more personal and intellectual are left unattended to.

ᕫ **Emotional Insensitivity**

By being totally focused on getting a job done, the hyperfocused *Gevurah* personality can be extremely effective in managing all the necessary steps to reach their goal; however, they may easily lack the emotional sensitivity to others in the process. They may realize the importance of caring for others, but once they step onto the battlefield of accomplishment, it may be very difficult to avoid trampling on the hearts of people whose involvement may impinge their ultimate achievement. When the *Gevurah* personality lacks a balanced dose of *chessed*, it is easy for such insensitivities to take hold.

ᕫ **Closed-Mindedness**

Gevurah personalities have a tendency to be skeptical about anything that they cannot see or touch in a concrete way. All the areas of open-mindedness that we saw in the *Chessed* personality are regarded as spacey and impractical to the *Gevurah* person. They need to see things in an organized and manageable form; otherwise, they are likely to feel uncomfortable and lacking the control that drives them toward their desired ends. Unfortunately, life's most important questions are often avoided as a result of this closed-mindedness. A person becomes obsessed with the details of accomplishment at the expense of being open to the spiritual dimension of life. To the *Gevurah* personality, what is eternal, ultimately meaningful, and most fulfilling in this world does not compare to the immediate sense of accomplishment achieved by being a workaholic. However, with even a small dose of the *Chessed* personality's open-mindedness, the strength of the *Gevurah* personality could be channeled toward a much more productive and fulfilling life.

⁓ Beauty Is for Those Who Have Nothing Better to Do with Their Time

Being inspired by the stunning world around us is a powerful means to connect to God. Taking time to notice the masterpiece enables us to appreciate the artist. To the *Gevurah* personality, however, enjoying the scenery is primarily for the passengers, not the driver, whose concentration must be on the road. And while that may be true when safety is at stake, the *Gevurah* personality easily goes overboard, and overlooks the beauty all around him even while at rest. A few minutes of looking at a beautiful sunset, a blossoming flower or a high-soaring bird could add a powerful dimension to his or her life, without significantly delaying his journey. Without such moments, these expressions of God's genius and creativity will be left unnoticed.

Journal

1. Which of the positive qualities of the *Gevurah* personality do you find within yourself? Rate how strong they manifest.

2. Which of the weaknesses of the *Gevurah* personality do you find within yourself?

_____

_____

_____

_____

_____

_____

_____

_____

_____

_____

_____

_____

_____

_____

_____

The *Tiferes* Personality

I glanced at my watch and walked a little faster. Jake was usually on time, but that wasn't why I was hurrying. He was very forgiving of lateness and always carried a book or some other way to pass the time. He was an incorrigible eavesdropper and constantly engaging total strangers in conversation, or more accurately, butting in and continuing whatever it was they had been discussing. Somehow, he always got away with it. I was in a hurry because I really needed to talk and Jake was an important set of ears. He really listened. He was a student of life and could see every problem from twelve different angles. As expected, he was already sitting in the café, but his chair was turned around and he was in deep discussion with a young couple at the next table.

When he saw me, he turned his chair around and rose to greet me.

"Hi, friend." Something about the way he said it warmed my heart and calmed me down. "How are things? How are the wife and family?"

"Well..." I hesitated. I had planned on having a pleasant conversation before burdening him with the real purpose of the meeting. "Actually, there's a problem." I began to tell him what was bothering me, going into more detail about my family problems than I had intended. His eyes never left my face and I knew he was listening deeply, paying attention to my every word.

When I finished, he sat back and sipped his tea. He drank Earl Grey with cream and sugar, a holdover habit from when he studied in England. "That's quite a tricky little predicament you've got there. Even if I wasn't so emotionally invested in you as a friend, I would find this compelling."

He thought for a few minutes before speaking. He began to apply theories and philosophies to my situation. At first I was a bit put off, feeling as though he were analyzing me like a lab rat, but eventually I realized that much of what he was saying was accurate and helpful. And more importantly, it was clear that he actually cared. The conversation got more complex as we delved deeper into the issue at hand. After a long discussion, it was time for me to leave. As I left, I looked back and saw my friend, Jake, still pondering.

The patriarch Jacob was the embodiment of *tiferes*, which means beauty and harmony. He drew upon the traits of his father and grandfather, and combined them in a balanced and healthy way. There are several other traits also associated with Jacob. One is that of compassion, inasmuch as compassion reflects a balanced approach in relating to others—not too much *chessed* and giving, which can overwhelm the recipient, and not too much *gevurah* and withholding, which can limit the kindness one shows another. Rather, compassion means relating and giving to others precisely what they need, when they need it and how they need it.

✌ Are You a *Tiferes* Personality?

As we did with *chessed* and *gevurah*, we will now examine some of the ways in which the *Tiferes* personality expresses themselves in the behavioral and emotional realm. Ask yourself if the following strengths and weaknesses sound familiar—this will help you take a step closer to the real you.

⁓ A World of Truth

Tiferes is usually considered to be a combination of *chessed* and *gevurah*, which is reflected in its balanced perspective and level of objectivity that is not swayed by the more radical traits of *chessed* and *gevurah*. This explains why Jacob also represents truth and the study of Torah (which is the ultimate truth). The Torah speaks of him as a scholar who dwelled in the tents of the study hall. As we will discuss later, the Hebrew word for truth, *emes*, is made up of the first, middle and last letter of the Hebrew alphabet, א-מ-ת, and refers to that which is constant and stable. Jacob represents the Torah scholar in his quest for the one, unwavering truth that stretches from beginning to end. Without *tiferes*, a person's ideas and actions may be imbalanced; the product of an overabundance of one of the personality types we discussed above. Partially formulated or imbalanced theories are dangerous in that they can cause people to dedicate their lives to goals that only distance them from their true purpose of meaning and pleasure. If a person is to survive the numerous challenges that regularly try to confuse our views on life, the truth and objectivity of *tiferes* is critical.

⁓ Appreciating the Mind

The *Tiferes* personality lives mostly in his mind. He is fascinated by ideas and deeply bothered when things don't make sense. He tends to be more entertained by philosophical discussions than other forms of leisure and entertainment. Although the *Tiferes* personality derives the greatest pleasure from Torah study, they are also drawn toward other areas of study. Science, in its quest to understand the true nature of the physical world; medicine and mental health to understand the inner workings of man; technology and engineering for its understanding and application of theoretical concepts. Even those philosophical discussions that have no apparent practical implication are captivating to the mind and heart of the *Tiferes* personality. Just give them a mind-twisting quiz and watch them get pulled into trying to unravel it. And of course, don't give them the answer or you will ruin all the fun.

✎ Inventive Creativity

The clear-thinking mind of the *Tiferes* personality has a natural talent for discovering new ways of using the various elements in the world. Finding a cure for illnesses or developing new inventions in hardware and software technology are accomplished by minds that are not afraid to delve deep into the inner makings of how things work and how to improve them.

The clear sense of judgment and balance in the *Tiferes* personality provides stability in their personal and family life. When there are challenges that need clear answers, they can usually be found in the *Tiferes* personality.

In business, the *Tiferes* personality exhibits the ability to think out of the box with creative yet realistic ideas and formulates the necessary strategies that a company needs to move forward by leaps and bounds.

✎ Hatred of Hypocrisy

The love of truth found in the *Tiferes* personality causes them to react instinctively against the types of hypocrisy that many people live with. Lying strikes a raw nerve. Conflicting ideas are intolerable. The *Tiferes* personality is always attuned to the consistency of ideas. You can easily spot them wherever you find people discussing theoretical issues. Even if the discussion was over some minor point, if the *Tiferes* personality overhears it, he will inevitably butt in to clear up any confusion. "I'm sorry to interfere, but what you are saying is absolutely wrong, for you said 'A' and he said 'B', and both of you are missing an important piece of this equation. Perhaps you should do a little more research in order to have such a discussion." In other words, next time you have a discussion, watch out for who may be listening in.

~ Less Vulnerable to Social Pressure

The *Tiferes* personality often prides themselves on their independent thinking. While the world around them follows trends and social pressures, they are the first to reject them. Even trends that are not necessarily damaging are initially regarded with suspicion, until their true value can be discerned. This independence provides a sense of stability in their journey through life, as they are not easily thrown off course by other people. The clarity gained in the formulation of a vision provides the strength to survive the lower points in their travels without losing sight of what truly matters. As we will discuss later, this ability to prioritize is an essential skill to develop on our journey.

~ Open to Spirituality

The more someone is searching for truth, the more they will inevitably look within the realm of spiritually. How can you claim to have looked honestly at the makeup of this world without exploring what is at the root of what makes us human? Although this may not be a quick intuitive process, the *Tiferes* personality is gifted in the deductive reasoning that leads him to see the Creator behind the creation, the soul within the human and the Godliness within all existence. Whereas the *Chessed* personality might sense this by looking at a beautiful sunset, the *Tiferes* personality's overwhelming search for truth leads them beyond the pragmatic approach of the scientific world, to find the very source of the brilliant design that constitutes our universe.

~ Tiferes Overboard

Balance, clarity, a love of truth—these are all the qualities that help a person maintain a sense of their positive attributes.

So where is there room for the *Tiferes* personality to go over-board? The answer is that because the balance between *chessed* and *gevurah* is maintained in the mind, the *Tiferes* personality runs the risk of leaving all of his understanding solely in the mind, without it influencing his heart and actions. It is easy for a *Tiferes* personality to see their own mind as a destination of its own, and begin to lose an awareness of the world around them. While their minds are busy in their brilliant thoughts, a little nerd is born. They no longer take care of their clothing; they forget to groom their hair. You can easily spot them, with one side of their shirt tucked in, and the other hanging out. And if their glasses break, and they don't have time to go to the local optometrist to fix them, a piece of tape is good enough. (Perhaps they never even noticed the optometrist around the corner, because their minds were too busy figuring out some new theory as they walked by.)

❦ Arrogance

If *you* were walking around with a clearer picture of life than most of the people you know, there is a good chance that you would start to feel a bit superior. This is one of the biggest traps for the *Tiferes* personality, because he starts to lose a sense of objectivity—which was his greatest trait. His greatest vulnerability is the one that eats away at the essence of his primary strength. Once his ego has taken control, the *Tiferes* personality is no longer an objective representation of truth and balance. Protecting his reputation becomes more important than what is right or caring. If you find yourself struggling with your ego in the realm of knowledge and intellectual authority, you are most likely a *Tiferes* personality. With a little work on humility and the integration of more *chessed* and *gevurah*, you will be able to remove the layers covering the great potential of your *Tiferes* soul.

Journal

1. Which of the positive qualities of the *Tiferes* personality do you find within yourself?

2. Which of the weaknesses of the *Tiferes* personality do you find within yourself?

3. Based on what you wrote at the end of the last three chapters, which personality did you have the most in common with?

4. Which personality did you have the least in common with?

Secondary Personalities

Still having a hard time finding your place in the inner world? Can't or don't want to peg yourself as one type or the other? You're right. Nothing is that simple, and no person can be completely defined as one of these three traits. In addition, Judaism teaches us that a healthy person integrates all three personality traits. Thus, most people have a secondary and perhaps even tertiary personality type that also plays a powerful influence in their lives. Unlike your primary personality type, which is driven by a higher connection to the higher level of your soul (*neshamah*), the secondary personality is rooted in the lower level. For example, you can have a primary personality of *Chessed* and a secondary personality of *Gevurah*. It is important to watch yourself and take note of when you get inspired toward more spiritual activities. Do you naturally stop to notice a sunset or a beautiful flower? Are you more drawn toward analyzing how this world works?

Also take note of when it initially seems very difficult to get yourself up and dedicate yourself to do something that is not in the area of your primary personality. For example, let's say you are a *Chessed* personality and love to hang out with people, but today you are feeling a bit too tired or even lazy. Then you hear of an opportunity to pack and distribute food packages to the homes of many poor people. Unlike a typical case of *chessed*, in this case you will so busy working behind the scenes that you will not have any direct involvement with the recipients. Yet, a voice of *gevurah* is heard from within and you are ready to go without any need for convincing. Had someone presented you with a good book to read, you may have fallen asleep after a few pages but something about being active and productive got you moving. Even if you could have read a book to research a way to help others, it still would not have been enough to get you out of your tired or lazy mood because you needed to be motivated by your secondary personality to get moving.

To help identify your primary and secondary personality please see the quiz in the appendix of this book. The questions should help you zoom in closer to the root of your soul's personality.

Hello Stranger

The next stop in our journey is actually your own home. But rather than looking at your home in the way you usually do, we are going to try to see it as if you were a total stranger. When you walk into someone else's house, you can't help but make certain assumption about them based on what they chose to hang on the walls, what types of things they spend their money on, how neat or messy the place is and numerous other subtleties that formulate a first impression of them.

Similarly, we are now going to create a picture album of our lives by taking a closer look at the surroundings that we have created for ourselves. Every choice we have made, every purchase and what we do with our possessions; all of these tell a story about the inner world that has been expressing itself through our outer actions.

Not only do we consciously and subconsciously build the world that we live in from day to day, but we are also screening out many options. The result is that we have created for ourselves our own little bubble of familiarity and pattern that is profoundly designed by our inner soul. Much like an artist who expresses their inner self through whatever external medium they are skilled to use, our little world is a powerful reflection of so much about us. It is like an extension of our soul being expressed through the world that we create.

Our surroundings therefore provide an incredible opportunity to examine the choices we have made to learn about the one inside who has made them. There is so much of our personality painted all over the walls of our individual bubbles that we have created for ourselves.

⟜ Now It's Time to Look at It

The first step is to put on the viewing glasses, change our mindset to see ourselves as if it were the first time, much like you would do with a stranger creating a first impression. The more we see the other person's environment, the more we solidify our assumptions or refine them with new insight. Similarly, when looking at your own little world, try to use the same explorative mind, but before you draw any conclusions just look around and soak it all in.

Next, take a few moments to appreciate that although in our journey we are working to discover what the best next step to take is, really you have already made many life choices. The world around you reflects everything you have created so far. That means that you have demonstrated the ability to guide yourself on the journey until now. Some of the choices may have been good while others not as productive, but there is certainly much to pat yourself on the back about. The skills we are trying to develop are just a finetune to enable you to identify the better choices more accurately and to get more out of each step along the way.

Without labeling or judging yourself, see what you have created. See the extension of your soul being expressed through your personal world. Are there patterns you notice about what you own? What have you shown to be your priorities? Do you find yourself spending money on things that serve one side of your life more than others? What do you seem to always have available (stuff you can't live without) and what do you tend to ignore? What type of feeling do you get from looking at it like a stranger?

Now start to use your judgmental eye to evaluate what your possessions are actually saying. Do you think it is wise spending or should you be more concerned about other things? Have you deprived yourself of things that would have contributed more to your life but you were too frugal or afraid to acquire?

Besides your actual possessions, the way you maintain them also tells a big part of the story. Is your world a neat and orderly world or is it in a constant state of messiness? Perhaps you like it neat but it takes a hyperfocused cleanup to get things organized once a month. Are there incomplete plans and designs for too many projects to ever achieve? Do you cherish your book collection or is your heart more connected to the furniture, pictures on the wall or perhaps the quilt cover on your bed? What kind of pictures do you have on the walls, if any? Are there pictures of people, scenery or perhaps more intriguing scenes of places or objects?

∼ Whose World Is This?

With this picture in mind, ask yourself if this is more of a world of a *Chessed*, *Gevurah* or *Tiferes* personality. *Chessed* personalities tend to be messier with lots of color and pictures of people and beautiful nature. *Gevurah* personalities are generally very neat and organized. There must be space on the wall more for functionality than for beauty. *Tiferes* is also found to be messy but more because of the distraction of interesting projects and research than because of people.

Regardless of whether or not you can see one of the primary personalities showing through your little world, you can still form a rich impression of your personality with its strengths and weaknesses. If you find this difficult to do, you may find it easier to start by looking at other peoples' worlds with an eye out for the parallels between the personalities you have gotten to know in others and their possessions. Then it will be easier to do this for yourself.

Who's the child in the faded photo
Wide eyes staring out the window
Taking in a brand new world
Where everything is ready to explore

Looking back I can see the me
The way I used to be[13]

The Home I Was Becoming

I had been living in a fairly small house in Toronto. For a person who leaned more toward the artsy side of life, the house looked rather bare and impersonal. Other than family photos, there were almost no pictures on the wall. The cheap furniture looked as if it had gone from borrower to borrower. Although this was not a reflection of my aesthetic taste, it was a reflection of the stage of life I was in. You see, after have lived some exciting years in Israel, my small family picked up to spend a short time in Toronto. It was going to be a short stay—six months to a year. Then it became two years, three years and yes, even a decade went by and we had yet to return to where our hearts longed to be—to Jerusalem, eye of the universe. Although we felt we were living in exile, our financial situation did get better. I had sold a technological innovation that put us in a position to buy a bigger house, while we still tried to decide if and when to move back to Israel. So in the eleventh year of life in Toronto, we moved into a house that was four times the size of the previous one

---

13. Verse from my song, "Watching the Time Go By."

(and ten times the size of our Jerusalem home). It had high ceilings, beautiful glass doors, wooden floors and a dream kitchen that matched the standards of any interior decorating magazine. We were living the dream of so many people.

But after a year of living there, we looked around at our possessions, the furniture and pictures on the wall. It was beautiful to the outside world, but it was a scary statement of contradiction with our inner world that was still thirsting for Jerusalem. Having our materialistic dreams fulfilled was just what we needed to wake us up to the inner voice that wanted to return home. Within a month, we packed up and moved back to Israel.

Sometimes we can learn from our surroundings to see who we are; sometimes we can learn from our surroundings who we are becoming.

What Am I Here to Achieve

"The starting point of a person's service is to recognize and reveal his prime characteristic and develop it to its completion through the paths of the Torah and be faithful to it. But he should not be satisfied with perfecting his natural trait since he is obligated to develop his other qualities in order to reach completion."[14]

Ask yourself, What am I living for? The Ramchal tells us one should answer as follows, "Our sages taught us that a person is created for the sole purpose of delighting in Hashem."[15] The question that most people still struggle with is: How am I as an individual supposed to achieve such a goal? Certainly God did not give me my strengths and weaknesses in order to do the same job as everyone else. After all we can find numerous examples of great righteous people who "delighted in Hashem" and yet still lived very different lives. So how is anyone supposed to figure out their true individual mission in this world?

Although we are conditioned to think in terms of what visible mark we can make on the world, the first place we must focus our efforts on is within our own character. The *Nesivos Shalom*

---

14. R. Eliyahu Dessler, *Michtav M'Eliyahu*, vol. II, p. 161.

15. R. Moshe Chaim Luzzato, *Mesillas Yesharim*, introduction.

suggests that we take one negative trait and one positive trait and make it our agenda to excel in both.

> *The first matter he needs to reflect deeply upon is his special mission in the world. Why has his soul come in to the world? The key to detecting his mission is that it is connected to his own root of wormwood and gall, which is the particular area in his personality that causes him the greatest difficulties and brings out the worst in him. The tzaddikim have said that his mission on earth is to correct precisely that area, and it is a mission that requires nothing short of total dedication. When it becomes clear to a person that his soul has descended for the purpose of rectifying this particular trait—that this is his mission on earth—no sacrifice is too dear for him. He will not let himself be deterred or distracted from expending every effort toward the fulfillment of his life's mission.*
>
> *The same idea applies concerning one's strengths. One needs to discern the special talents with which Hashem has bestowed him and through which he is given the opportunity to draw closer to Hashem. For God created this corresponding to that. In the same way that one has a particular negative trait, one also has a particular strength through which he can success-fully ascend spiritually. If one does not recognize his special strength, he is like a person blind in one eye that is exempt from the "viewing" sacrifice of pilgrimage. If someone is blessed with an exceptional talent in Torah, it is a sign that his mission is to succeed in Torah; if someone loves to be generous, it is a sign that this area is connected to the root of his soul.*[16]

If you try to address too many areas at one time you risk be-coming discouraged and abandoning the mission altogether. In fact there is a tremendous advantage to focusing on one negative

---

16. R. Shalom Noach Berezovsky, *Nesivos Shalom*, "Awareness," chapter 5.

trait and one positive one. This will serve as a tremendous focus to allow for personal growth in both areas. Not only will you enjoy further developing the natural talent that you so much enjoy, but it will provide you with the strength to conquer the worst of your flaws as well. It is not meant to be a quick, easy fix. In some cases, it can be a lifetime mission. But that is the reason why you were given the challenge. And even though people won't clap and pay large sums for such an achievement, in God's eyes, you have done what you were created to do.

> *"What is the straight path that one should cling to?"*[17]
> *Rabbeinu Yonah explains that obviously a person should cling to all their good character traits. But what the Mishnah means is that a person should choose a particular trait that is best for them to advance forward with. It is through the progress one makes on a trait that they are likely to access that they will find the strength and passion to apply to other traits that are less natural.*

With the right attitude, one can apply the same enthusiasm to ones choice of negative quality by remembering that true success in life is working on what God considers to be valuable. In addition, the increase of positive energy through allowing more room in your life for your primary positive trait, will serve as a powerful motivator to assist in overcoming the negative trait as well.

> *One of the profound truths in creation would seem to be that each man's nature fits his task in life so that it is specifically his best natural quality that can overcome the most basic fault that he has. One who succeeds in grasping his chief quality and knowing his chief fault has attained a tremendous thing, for now he knows what God asks from him.*[18]

---

17. *Ethics of the Fathers* 2:1.
18. R. Shlomo Wolbe, *Alei Shur*, vol. I, p. 146, based on R. Yerucham Levovitz.

Travelers Tale

When I was studying music composition at Indiana University, I had the amazing opportunity of booking a recording studio once a week. I usually booked it at around six p.m. so no one could take any later slot. When I starting recording I was often very tired from a full day of studies and usually did not eat a proper dinner before going. Yet a new source of energy took over my mind, body and soul. I was able to stay up the whole night creatively immersed in the form of art that I loved and seemed to love me. The next day I was completely wiped but, hey, it was well worth it. Today, as a Torah observant Jew, I have a recording studio in my home here in Israel. It is an essential part of my spiritual diet and it helps my Torah learning, prayer and overall feeling of being alive. In fact a great rabbi, R. Abraham Twerski, told me that I must spend twenty percent of my time working on my music.

⁓ Choose Your Battles

In order to decide what positive area to focus on, let's try to use the picture of yourself that you have developed so far. If you were able to see yourself fitting into one of the three primary personality types, ask yourself which aspect of the personality is your strongest attribute, both in terms of what you enjoy and in terms of how much it can be expressed in a positive way. For example, you may find that there is an activity that drives you with a much higher level of motivation than any other. This would give you so much positive energy that, if you could, you would spend the majority of your time doing it. But if it doesn't contribute to your life, family or community, it is not going to serve your higher ideals. For example, you may love taking walks in the forest but it is not something you can base most of your life upon unless you find some creative way to use it to help people in a meaningful way. On the other hand, if you love making people smile, doing acts of *chessed*, enriching people with wisdom or creating systems to improve the way people live, it doesn't take much to find ways of using such passions.

You can use the tools we have discussed so far to try to zoom in on what you truly have a passion to do while enabling yourself to do what is meaningful. (In Part Two, as we explore the anatomy of the soul, we will discuss what makes something sincerely meaningful.) Try to design a way to use that passion in more areas of your life—in a formal setting, such as a career or volunteer, or in informal settings, such as how you deal with people in your life.

If you are still having a hard time deciding on a positive virtue to work with, it may help to look at the following list.

Chessed-Related Qualities

- Appreciates the beauty in nature and art
- Enjoys helping others
- Enjoys people
- Is able to live in the moment
- Is easily forgiving of others
- Is generous
- Is good at making friends
- Is naturally very kind
- Is optimistic
- Makes people feel loved and cared for
- Tunes into the feelings of others; can communicate to their emotional needs

Gevurah-Related Qualities

- Enjoys leadership

- Is a good disciplinarian
- Is a good team player
- Is courageous to fight for the right cause
- Is responsible to the community
- Is well disciplined
- Looks out for fairness
- Manages details very efficiently
- Takes initiative
- Takes responsibility

Tiferes-Related Qualities

- Applies ingenuity to solve problems
- Figures out how things work
- Has a love of learning
- Is able to dedicate attention to acquiring mass amounts of knowledge
- Is inspired by new ideas and experiences
- Is natural at learning new skills
- Thinks out of the box
- Thinks through ideas to come to a conclusion in a clear and rational way

✺ Negative Trait

Okay, now let's look at the negative trait to work on. Find something really bad. What is your biggest block? Some people know their block very clearly while other are completely oblivious to it. Here are some more hints as to how to find it:

One approach is to look at our primary attributes and match them with one of the three negative attributes stated in the following Mishnah: "Three things destroy the world, *kinah* (jealousy), *taavah* (lust) and *kavod* (ego) remove a person from the world."[19] This means that these things take control over your objectivity and cause you to make bad choices.

There were three destructive events in the world before Abraham, Isaac and Jacob came to rectify them. Cain killed his brother out of jealousy... Abraham's love and *chessed* was the opposite of *kinah*. The generation of Noah became completely perverted and immersed in lust. Jacob's purity of Torah and *tiferes* was the rectification for the lust. As they say, "A *daf* a day (a page of Talmud) keeps the *yetzer hara* (evil inclination) away." Nimrod built the tower of Bavel to show his egotistical might over God. Isaac's humility and *gevurah* was the opposite of *kavod*. Your weakest of the positive trait may be a hint to your negative trait. For example if you are very weak in the positive attribute of *chessed*, you should ask yourself if you are prone to jealousy. The last thing a jealous person wants to do is give to someone else, especially the one they are jealous of. Ask yourself which of these three you are most vulnerable to and how much that negative trait controls your life.

If you still have not found the troublemaker in you, don't worry there are plenty more to consider.

Another way to figure out the negative trait to work on is simply by asking someone you trust to be really honest about what they think would be the most important attribute to work on.

Think about people who really get on your nerves. The thing that bothers you about them often reflects a weakness in yourself. People who are over punctual bother people who need to learn how to be. People who are annoyed by people who are too laidback also need to learn how to relax more. Try it.

Look at the time when you felt like the biggest failure and try to find a pattern that led you to such an error. You didn't know

---

19. *Ethics of the Fathers* 6:21.

when to stop talking, your jealousy got control of you or anger made you say things you should not have said. Was that a one-time mistake or a repeating pattern in your life—in which case it is well-worth working on?

◟ Make It Part of Your Daily Life

Once you have figured out your most positive and negative battles, then it's time to look at your schedule and lifestyle and reevaluate if you are allowing yourself enough time to express the positive. If you get enough pleasure from your positive trait it will make it much easier to tackle the negative one. Remember, this is what God wants of you and therefore well-worth a large amount of time in your day to develop to the next level.

In the second part of this book, as we learn to become more aware of the soul, we will discover that negative behaviors are merely an identification with the drives of the body. The more we drive home this awareness into our minds and hearts, the quieter the voice of the *yetzer hara* becomes, and selfishness, anger, jealousy and many other negative behaviors become more manageable.

In the chapter, "Spiritual Self-Defense," we will discuss more ways to build a strategy to fight this battle.

◟ True Success

Once you have created a battle plan you must cherish it. It is your way of achieving God's will in this world. You must find ways to appreciate every little step of growth along the way. The more you can define your mission and identify what level you are on, the easier it will be to appreciate your success.

The problem is that you will need to be strong to fight the voices of the world that only defines success based on external matters. There are plenty of miserable "successful" people out there. So you have to hold on tight to the Jewish understanding of success. Remember, your goal is to use your strengths and weaknesses to come close to God.

When you know what your true mission is, you will see your success as long as you don't need to display it to others. For example, while working on improving a negative trait, you may have times when you fall. Your ability to lift yourself back up and not allow a fall to destroy your attitude is a great accomplishment. Yet to any outsider there is nothing different than the day before. Here is a more mystical understanding of what takes place when we fall and lift ourselves back up.

> *The reason for the constant spiritual upheavals that take place in a person's life is that one's mission is to descend to the lower levels in order to refine and elevate them. This allows the sparks of holiness trapped in those levels to be released and restored to their proper place.*
>
> *This should teach you how careful one should be not to become embittered about the spiritual lot God has bequeathed him, whether small or great. Or if one feels that he is not as successful in spiritual matters as he should be, or if he feels that he has more challenges dealing with his evil inclination than he should have [he should not become bitter]. For one can never know what task he was sent into this world to perform. One person may have been sent to [metaphorically] clean the gutters, to purify them of all pollution and is constantly in a position of unease and constriction, while another was sent to adorn the king's chambers and make a crown upon his head, and thereby enjoys all of the comforts of royalty at all times.*
>
> *Thus one's heart should never sink because of life's vicissitudes; rather he should constantly strengthen himself. Only God knows the secrets of His plans, giving each individual the appropriate tasks, allowing each individual to repair his supernal*

root; and together everyone shall bask in the light of the Living God.[20]

～ Mission Possible

There are certain options in life that are clearly not meant for certain people. Even if something seems exciting to your personality, it does not mean that it is what you should spend your energy trying to achieve. I am not saying that you shouldn't think big. Great accomplishments start with great visions. But it is important to recognize that some things are just completely impractical. For example, someone who has a physical disability was not meant to run in the regular Olympics. Someone who is tone deaf was not meant to be a singer. Accepting God-given restrictions can redeem you from the pressure of having to play a role that is not meant for you to play. In fact, the weakness should help by pointing you toward your true positive attribute that should be expressed.

---

20. R. Shlomo Elyashiv, *Sefer Hadei'ah* 5:5:5.

Journal

Decide on one quality that you believe you have been blessed with and enjoy.

1. How do you think you can use this quality to accomplish the following:

   To personally better your life

   To help those who are closest to you

   To contribute to the community or the world in some way

2. How do you envision yourself after one year of having diligently including more of this quality in your life?

3. In order to achieve this level in one year, try to envision your milestones of

   Three months

   Six months

   Nine months

4. Decide on a day-to-day plan of action to make your three-month vision achievable

5. What negative trait would you like to make a priority to work to overcome?

6. How do you see your improvement in this area helping your life?

7. How do you envision yourself after one year of having diligently worked on overcoming this negative trait?

8. In order to achieve this level in one year, try to envision your milestones of

   Three months

   Six months

   Nine months

9. Decide on a day-to-day plan of action to make your three-month vision achievable.

How to Choose a Career

It's nice to talk about your identity and individuality, but what if you come up with the conclusion that you were brought into this world to be an artist but you don't see any way to secure your livelihood? True, many artists become teachers of art, but let's say that's not for you. You are not a teacher. You are an "artist." So what are you supposed to do now? Is the "real you" meant to starve to fulfill its inner purpose? Unfortunately, there are many activities that provide people with tremendous inspiration yet cannot be expressed in context of a career. Must they spend the majority of their life doing something that lacks personal connection?

If you look closer at your talents, you will find that there is something much deeper that defines who you are than being an artist or whatever other talent you have identified with. At the root of your talents are qualities that help you as an artist but are in no way limited to that one form of expression. For example, I am a musician. When I was in music school I thought that the only career that I could go into was music. But if you would have compared my personality and skill set with other music students you would have found a world of difference. I was not a performer. I was a composition major. I spent most of my time putting together the pieces of a big puzzle in a way that would sound good. The performers were taking other people's music and trying to express it as beautifully as possible. These are two different worlds.

My natural talents were actually noticeable as a little kid when I used to sit on the floor working on three puzzles at the same time. When my mother would ask me to clean up one of the puzzles, I told her that I wasn't finished because I was just working on another one and was coming back to the first one later. That is what I do when I write a few songs in the same time period, or a few chapters of a book or invent products to patent. These are all activities that come out of the same basic love of putting the pieces together in a creative and communicative way.

When you are trying to decide on a career, you must be flexible to see where you can apply your root personality and skills beyond the limited applications and jobs that are predefined by society. We are too quick to say that if you are good at writing music, you should be a composer. That may be true in cases where there is a promising way to make a living from it, but for many, it is just a hint to an underlying talent that can be applied to something that can be just as pleasurable and financially more secure. So try to take what you have learned about yourself and separate it from any career definitions. Then use this clear picture of the root of your soul's personality and explore what career options will provide for a good opportunity to utilize your gifted skills.

R. Bachye Ibn Pakudei, in *Duties of the Heart*, suggests the following to help figure out if a career is suitable for you.

> *The **affinity** one has toward a particular vocation is a Divine signal pointing him in that direction. Each person has a natural **inclination** toward a specific area of work more than another; for God has imprinted this affinity into each person's nature... When one finds within himself a **desire** for a particular type of pursuit, and believes that he is well-suited for it, he should **invest** himself in that pursuit and use it as a means for earning a livelihood. And he should not give up that pursuit when*

*at times he fails to support himself; rather he should **trust in
God** that He will give him enough to live all the days of his life.*[21]

The above lesson from *Chovos HaLevavos* can be summarized by
remembering the five words in bold.

1. **Affinity**—make sure you will use your true natural talents.

2. **Inclination**—you feel a preference toward this type of work.

3. **Desire**—you can envision getting day-to-day enjoyment
   from the work.

4. **Invest**—you believe in the potential and suitability enough
   that you will be willing to invest a lot of time and effort into
   it.

5. **Trust in God**—*emunah* that Hashem will provide you with
   your livelihood especially during the low times when it looks
   like you will not succeed.

Try to take what you have learned about your personality
and ask yourself if your choice of career can live up to these five
requirements. In addition to the specifics of the career, there are
always great opportunities to develop a closer relationship with
God through the daily challenges faced in the business world. Being honest, greeting people in a pleasant way and knowing that
your product can be of benefit to people's lives in some way, are
only a few of the considerations that shape the holiness that one
brings into their career.

> *In God's world, there is nothing or no type of pursuit that is
> devoid of holiness. Wherever refined character traits, kindness
> and love of fellow man can be found, the work being done is
> elevated to the level of Divine service!*

---

21. *Chovos HaLevavos*, "Gate of Trust," chap. 3.

Each vocation brings its own store of challenges, whether it be the temptation to overcharge or underpay, the difficulty of always keeping one's word, making sure to avoid selling forbidden things or avoiding unacceptable business tactics, etc. When a Jew encounters such a situation, he must know that this is his mission —to rise to the occasion and observe the halachah [law].[22]

As we discussed in context of developing our traits, success is not to be measured by how the world defines us. We must hold on tight to our inner visions and goals. Once we place ourselves within the business world, this becomes even more challenging because the definition of success is so easily swayed by external values and social pressure. This can not only damage our productive path in life, but it can also cause us to make bad business judgment and cloud our self-awareness.

So, besides the effort required to choose the right career, we must be well prepared to hold onto the "real you" while in the business world. As we will see, a powerful tool to prepare oneself for this challenge is presented in the upcoming chapter, "Spiritual Self-Defense."

---

22. R. Shlomo Wolbe, *Alei Shur*, vol. II, p. 270.

Lessons of Excellence

O ne of the greatest ways to fix your weakness is by learning from people who are very different from you. For example, if you are weak at self-motivation and discipline, learn from the ways of a *Gevurah* personality. Many people avoid people who are different from them, but they actually hold the key to repairing the very thing that could transform their life.

By now, you have learned to identify the primary personality types and hopefully, you have even gotten a sense of where you belong in this big picture. Perhaps you recognized yourself in the descriptions, or perhaps you recognized your friends. One of the surest ways for a person to know about himself is to consider with whom he spends his free time. Are your friends all neat and orderly, punctilious and overly courteous, like the *Gevurah* personality, or are they relaxed and artistic, like the *Chessed* person?

The point of this book, however, is not merely to learn more about yourself, but also to grow. And there is no surer way of growing than by incorporating different and foreign personality traits into your existing spiritual and emotional makeup. By doing so, we develop a more balanced life, and do not fall into the trap of expressing one trait without boundaries which leads to the negative repercussions of personality "overload" that we've discussed. An explorative traveler not only visits different parts of a land, but learns something from the people and culture that he could take home with him. As important as it is to know what is at the root of your soul, it is also critical to make sure that you have a good amount of the other two personality's qualities integrated into your life.

This is the best part of traveling: meeting new people, experiencing new things, and, of course, integrating all those new experiences into our lives. Thus, I have chosen an example of a powerful attribute from each of the personality types to help out the others. From the *Chessed* personality, we will learn the skill of appreciating people who are different than us. *Gevurah* will give us the skills to fight off the internal enemy that tries to push us off track and *Tiferes* will supply us with the skills to find balance and objectivity. Although above we have listed many qualities of each personality type, we are going to focus on one critical quality that can serve as a powerful lesson from each.

Acknowledging Others: Brought to You by the Chessed Personality

The admirable quality of being accepting and loving of others seems to be so natural to the *Chessed* personality that other people are convinced that it was meant only for them. When the *Chessed* personality meets new people, they become alive, no matter how different the others may be. Yet, non-*Chessed* people often feel a sense of distance and discomfort when they meet people who demonstrate a different way of thinking, acting or dressing.

If you identify with the latter judgmental trait, the question to ask is how you can learn to accept others with a sense of warmth and love. Actually, you can do this without losing a sense of who you really are. For instance, if you are a good judge as to whether you can trust people or not, which is a *Gevurah* trait, you can still learn to be warm and caring.

For instance, remember that just as you were brought into this world with a natural set of personality strengths, so was everyone else. God, who is just, has blessed other people with qualities that are right for them, just as He blessed you. When you appreciate these qualities, you are appreciating their nature as Divine gifts. They are not the invention of the person whom you find difficult to like. These qualities are an essential part of their soul. In this way, you temper your criticism with a dose of love and acceptance.

Second, even when the other type of person is not thoroughly balanced in their life and are too extreme in their particular personality trait, if you remember that this is a very common error, it will become much easier to accept. Just as you understand a person who is imbalanced in your personality type, you can understand how a person with a different personality can become unbalanced in a different direction—even though you don't easily relate to that trait, and it appears to you to be far more inappropriate.

Another important principle in loving people who are different is to know that you can love them even if they are "crazy" in your eyes. Why must they be the same type as you to be worthy of being cared for? For your sake and theirs, going outside of your comfort zone and relating to the beauty in a different type of person is a much greater act of love than caring for people who are like you. Listen when that inner voice starts to become critical of the other person. Before you fabricate an excuse to avoid them, think about the opportunity to explore new territory in your personality, utilize your inner strength to reject negative thoughts and enjoy the challenge of such a growing expression of real love.

Another important tool is to begin by watching how a *Chessed* personality acts with others, and then imitate them, until you become good at it yourself. At first, it may feel artificial, but if you persevere, it will become part of your personality. Enjoy the "people person" dormant within you. The occasional cup of wine shows us that there is a much more sociable loving side to the introvert that enjoys coming out. This is something we can work on without the need for wine.

To develop the skills to love others, it's good to remember that we all have a share of all three personalities inside of us. We are trying to achieve the natural *Chessed* part of who you are. The more you express it, the more you will become familiar and comfortable with that part of you that usually gets covered up by your dominant personality strengths. But even your primary strengths will be expressed much more with the expression of your complementary traits. It is spiritually very healthy to build this stability of expression and thereby become a more balanced and happy person.

Spiritual Self-Defense: Brought to You by the Gevurah Personality

The natural skills of the *Gevurah* personality are trained to counter spiritual challenges, much in the same way that martial arts masters are disciplined for self-defense. Although when we watch people use karate or other forms of martial arts, we tend to see the kicks, punches and blocks in their entirety without picturing the numerous elements that have been woven together to be able to perform so effectively in response to their opponent. Breathing, balance, self-awareness and a strong sense of spatial judgment are needed just to get started. Each kick is composed of a number of stages that had to be practiced on their own and then together within numerous drills which eventually link together into routines. When suddenly being attacked in a dark alley, our martial artist doesn't stop to evaluate which move to make next. Rather, they have developed "automated response" by having repeatedly drilled the reflexive response into their "muscle memory" in the practice studio. The flash of a punch speeding toward them triggers a block and counter response within a fraction of a second.

"One who follows his own straightness is a God-fearing person."[23] *Since people have different character traits, each individual is prone to sinning in certain areas more than others. Therefore, a person must develop his own path, erecting safeguards for himself in the areas that he is more vulnerable, although others who do not face the same struggles will not need those safeguards. This is the idea of "following his own straightness," i.e., following one's own straight path. One who does this, in spite of the fact that others who do not understand his reasons frown upon his ways, is truly God-fearing.*[24]

This is a natural talent for the *Gevurah* personality. Once they have made a plan in life, their choices are solid and they are ready to move forward at full steam. They are well-prepared for most of the challenges that are inevitably going to try to attack them in the dark alleys of life.

On the other hand, such structured behavior is anathema to the *Chessed* personality, who prefers spontaneity and a lack of discipline. However, that attitude leaves them vulnerable to attacks of the evil inclination. Rather than fight it, they tend to go with the flow.

Thus, in order to be prepared for the various battles of life, one has to work hard to exercise our *gevurah*, to bring our choices to the "muscle reflex" level of awareness and preparedness. There are many destructive internal voices that work so hard to limit our potential, using a variety of offensive techniques. We must become aware of them and respond instinctively, if we are to win the battle. We must therefore learn what we can about the moves of the enemy, while practicing the drills that we will need to use in the battle. Let's look at a few techniques that our *Gevurah* personality can offer.

---

23. Proverbs 14:2.

24. Vilna Gaon on ibid.

⌁ To Fight or Not to Fight

The *Gevurah* personality knows when to attack and when to avoid a challenge. That's the first rule of martial arts, as well. Don't get in a fight. (But if you are already in a fight, make sure you don't lose.) There is no point in placing yourself in a difficult situation just to pass the test of saying no; it is a bigger achievement to humbly avoid the challenge, and not risk losing.

Let's imagine that you are on a strict diet. Today, you have an appointment about five blocks from your house. There are two ways to get there. The shorter way takes you past your favorite ice cream store, and the longer way does not. However, you already know that when you walk by the shop, a little voice will start chattering in your head, explaining to you why you must have an ice cream. "No problem," you say to yourself, "I'll just walk by. It's not hard suppressing my desire for the most delicious dessert in the world." And so you take the short ice-cream route. Although you decided not to go in, on your way to the appointment, just as you pass by the store you don't plan to visit, you feel the need use the bathroom, and of course it's impossible to wait even five more minutes until you get to your destination. You know they wouldn't mind you using their restroom, so you go in. But then, your sense of guilt and moral responsibility tells you that you really should buy an ice cream to compensate them. And even though you could also order a bottle of spring water, your favorite treat is staring at you in the face. What would you do? Will you feel a tremendous surge of *gevurah* to battle the enemy or will the confrontation you created for yourself convince you to indulge?

This is only an example of the many battles that we can choose to avoid if we exercise our *gevurah* before we enter the danger zone. The humility to know your weaknesses is key to preventing such confrontations. Joseph exercised this quality when he ran away from the wife of Potiphar even though she had grabbed hold of a piece of his clothing that she could use to falsely prove him guilty of being the seducer. She was hoping that he would go back to get it, but knowing that he was too vulnerable kept Joseph away from the temptation, even at the expense of being thrown in jail for a crime he never committed. It is worth developing a clear list of vulnerabilities in order to know what battle to avoid wherever possible.

⌇ Review and More Review

Our martial artist did not watch a demonstration of kicks and blocks and then suddenly acquire the skill. It takes practice over and over again to get it right. So too, on the spiritual battlefront we need to learn the voices of the inner enemy and as soon as we hear it starting up a fight, we can be ready to block it as early as possible. This can only be achieved with a neat and organized list of your opponents and their arguments. That way when you face the enemy, you have a fighting chance. If this seems too out of character for you to develop, by developing these types of skills in the physical realm first, it will make it easier to apply to the spiritual battle. Consider self-defense, exercise or a sport that takes strong discipline and taste the same *gevurah* that should be applied on the inner court.

A Balancing Act:
Brought to You by the Tiferes Personality

Whether you are a *Chessed* personality or a *Gevurah* personality, there is an important lesson to learn from your friend, the *Tiferes* personality, as well. One of the most important qualities from this type of individual is balance. As we explained above, *tiferes* is born out of the combination and balance of *chessed* and *gevurah*. Biblically, this is personified by Jacob, who balanced the proclivities of his father and grandfather, Abraham and Isaac. How do we apply this in our lives? The very fact that we are open to learning from people different from us naturally creates a more balanced life. But there is another expression of the balance we can learn, which is the *Tiferes* personality's ability to face various challenges in life with the harmony of both the intellect and emotions.

For instance, how does the *Tiferes* personality deal with a difficult decision? First, they briefly scan the situation. They neither act nor respond until they have gathered enough information to assess what the real problem is that needs to be solved. Part of that assessment is also to feel out who is involved and what kind of emotional consequences are at stake. Feeling for those involved does not contradict their ability to act practically. They can maintain an emotional awareness and sensitivity, without allowing it to overwhelm their ability to maintain a cool sense of objectivity. This is challenging for the *Chessed* personality, who is prone to react too quickly out of empathy for others, and the *Gevurah* personality, who is likely to react too quickly out of a need to take action.

So, if you are not a *Tiferes* personality, you should devote your efforts to attaining this type of objectivity. Practice on small choices. When someone asks you a question, stop, think and try to get a feel for what emotions are behind the question being asked. Silence is golden. The person you are about to answer will appreciate the fact that you didn't rush into an answer, as though you need to prove that you are smart or capable. Pausing to think about the answer is always appreciated, and provides you more time to formulate a correct response. The same applies to personal decisions and challenges. Even when you hear a voice telling you what to do, stop, think, feel and then take action.

Tiferes people exude a sense of inner peace. They are not at war with themselves and their decisions. They have learned to trust their judgment, and do not project anxiety or uncertainty. Try to imitate such people. Find people who you think are blessed and refined with this quality. By acting like them, you will naturally start to create a sense of balance and harmony within your soul.

Preparing to Go Deeper

So you have met my three friends with all their strengths and weaknesses and now you hopefully have a stronger sense of your primary and secondary personality. Perhaps you are even getting clarity on what it is you are truly looking for as an individual both in terms of utilizing your talents and working to overcome your challenges. Keep it up.

But now we have arrived at the exciting turning point in our journey where we are about to go beyond defining the unique personality of your soul. We are going to travel deeper inland with the challenging goal of actually feeling the soul in an experiential way much like we do with our senses to connect to our surroundings.

Not only will this help you become a more spiritually aware person, but it will enable you to clearly hear and know when to trust that gut feeling inside when it is telling you to make an important choice in your life. The Torah view is that there is incredible truth being spoken from that inner voice. The problem is that it is far too easy to be convinced that what you desire for impure reasons is also being spoken from that point of truthful intuition. Later, in the chapter, "The Prophet Within," we will learn how to both hear what our gut is saying and how to cross-examine its authenticity so to prevent the dangers that could transpire should we go down the wrong road. But in order to reach such heights of awareness, we must first make sure that our minds are sensitized to notice the subtleties of the spiritual dimension of life. To help prepare us to go deeper, I would like to share the following thought inspired by R. Kalonymus Kalman Shapira of Piaseczna:

> *The general attribute of being an aware person is an essential requirement in the pursuit of self-awareness. Only someone who can trust in their mind's ability to assemble abstract information will be able to recognize the beauty of what they discover inside. This should not be discouraging because our minds regularly make incredible calculations based on very abstracts bits of information. The only problem is that our attitude of awareness chooses to apply this skill only to certain areas of life. This is apparent when driving a car, for example. Without much thought, the driver can evaluate and combine such details as distance, speed, the size of other objects and space available to move through and around traffic. Even though the slightest miscalculation could be dangerous, the average driver willingly makes life-threatening decisions based on thousands of short flashes of visual information. One does not need to have a mental picture of the entire road and all the cars in one's thoughts to drive safely. The mind begins to develop this ability from the time that we are children; that is, the ability to draw conclusions based upon fragments of information, a "slice" of the entire picture, as psychologists call it.*
>
> *Yet, despite the many areas of life where we are proficient in awareness, we do not always apply it to seeing our inner selves. Too often, for a variety of reasons, we filter out or lose trust in what we see and hear. It will require time and patience to hear your deep inner voice clearly. As you visit your inner world, you will want to take note of those things you encounter along the way. When you begin to notice something spiritual, you may also hear an opposing voice that tells you to dismiss it as being foolish and unscientific—unfit for rational people like you. Yet the same way that you drive a car based upon bits of information, so should you begin to develop a new sense of self,*

based upon small flashes of insight. Then, you will be opening the door to a whole new world inside.[25]

Can you hear the raindrops
Dancing on the rooftops
See the artist paint the shapes of time
You can see my thinking
Through the song I'm singing
If you see the world beyond your eyes
Let the child grow
Let the river flow
Let your heart go
Open up the windows of your mind[26]

25. Based on *Bnei Machshava Tova*, R. Kalonymus Kalman Shapira, Piaseczna Rebbe.

26. From my song, "Windows of Your Mind."

Part II
What Are
YOU?

What Is the Soul?

We are now going to travel into a different type of inner awareness. It's time to get to know and experience the soul, not just as a theoretical abstract concept but as something that you can sense—as you do when smelling a pleasant spice. Close your eyes and try to become aware of that conscious being inside of you. Ask yourself, "What is that living energy that you can't quite touch, yet it seems to be connected to your body?" (Okay, you can open your eyes now.)

The more we can heighten our awareness with that living being, the easier it is to live on a higher spiritual level. Therefore, the goal of Part Two of this book is not only to present a description of the soul, but also to explore inspirational ideas that will help us live with this heightened awareness from day to day. Not an easy challenge but worth every ounce of effort.

So let's begin with the big question: What are you? That's easy, you say. I'm a human being. But what constitutes a human being? Is it a soul? Is it a body? Is it both? That answer doesn't tell us much. How does that make you different than your pet dog? They also have a body and a soul. Dogs seem to have feelings and if you look at them in the eyes there seems to be something deeper than just a physical animal. So let's take a much closer look at the question of what makes up a human being.

It is clear that the answer to the question will have profound implications in almost every area of life. In fact, the answers to all the questions we have explored until now about our unique role in this world will be deepened by understanding the underlying question of what we are as human beings. A spiritually aware person is far more equipped to make individual life choices than someone who is out of touch with their soul. So as we continue our journey to getting to know the real you, our understanding of the intrinsic nature of the soul will strongly influence the specific discoveries we will ultimately make about our personality and our role in this world.

∽ YOU—Were Created in God's Image

Most people admit that a human being is more than a mere collection of atoms and molecules. That description may work for the body, but it's not going to help when trying to define that conscious being inside. The following verses in Genesis give the clearest answer: "So God created mankind in His own image; in His own image God created them; male and female He created them."[27]

This verse is teaching us that a human being is a reflection of God, made in the Divine image. But what does that mean? Because Judaism unequivocally states that God is not physical and has no image, the words cannot be referring to the human body. Yet this is perhaps the most important question that needs to be answered if we are to understand the true nature of the soul. Thousands of books, written by the greatest Torah scholars over many centuries, have addressed this topic.

Let's look at some of the explanations of what it means to be created in the image of God and how that affects our lives.

---

27. Genesis 1:27.

⌒ A Reflection of God's Free Will

According to many great Jewish thinkers, this God-like trait within us is our source to reason and to act freely based upon our choices. We understand that God totally transcends the world. As such, He is in no way subject to the conditions of the world. His every action is free and autonomous, flowing from His being in a way that is not contingent upon anything else. Amazingly, this can also be true for human beings. While it may seem that we are influenced by many exterior circumstances—our families, our jobs, our own bodies—to live as created in God's image is to realize that we, too, have complete freedom of will. We can use our intellect to consider every available option and then decide which one suits us best. Even when we are physically restricted in our options (such as a person in jail), our souls and spirits can always be free. We can reject our situation or concede to it. We can mentally fight against it or embrace it.

The Kabbalah
of Being Human

Man was not created for God to observe like a piece of art. We were created to have a loving relationship with our Maker. But how is it possible for a human being to relate to a totally abstract Being? The underlying principle within the deeper explanations of being created in God's image is that we have something God-like within us. As we are about to see, the way we were fashioned physically and spiritually is a figurative representative of what we have to learn about our Creator. Nothing about the design of the human body, heart and soul is just coincidental. Everything is on some level a reflection and lesson about how God operates in the world and how we are to relate to Him. Let's try to make some practical sense of this.

⮞ Blinded by the Light

To shed some light on this issue, imagine you are standing in the dark, in a parking lot. Suddenly, a car parked right in front of you turns on its lights, flashing its high beams directly in your eyes. What do you see? The answer, obviously, is nothing. You've been blinded—not by the dark, but by too much light. Ironically, if you were wearing a pair of sunglasses, you would have been able to see better. In other words, there are times that by reducing the amount of light, we actually can see more.

This same dynamic occurs in the relationship between God and the world. Whatever little we actually know about God, we can at least say that He totally transcends any limitations or forms of perception. Kabbalah refers to Him as the *Ein Sof*, meaning, the One without end. (*Sefer Yetzirah*, *Zohar* and many other sources) This is the very opposite of creation, which is limited and perceivable. Were God to shine the light of His essence into the world, no created being could possibly exist. We would be as negated as the light of a candle in the sun. It would be just too blinding.

However, God desired to create a world that could be inhabited by His creations, in which He could enter into a relationship with them. He also wanted man to play an active role in bringing the light of God into the physical world.

To this end, God diminished His infinite light and life force, in order to allow the world to exist as a seemingly independent entity. He created a system that works much like the resistors of a power plant. When the electrical plant wants to deliver power to a city, it does so via cables and resistors that lower the voltage that flows from the plant. Only because of that can you enjoy your toast and coffee each morning. But if you dare take your toaster to the power plant itself and plug it directly into the generator, not only will you not enjoy your toast, you might end up fried yourself.

So, too, with the creation of the world: in order for the world to exist, and not get fried, God shines His light down through a series of resistors and filters. On the one hand, these reduce the level of exposure of the Infinite Light, while on the other hand, it allows us humans to experience His presence in the world and serve Him. The challenge of life is not to be fooled by the darkness, but to look for the sparks of light that shine in it, and use them to connect back to our source.

~ Ten Steps Down

One of the most powerful ways to heighten our awareness of the soul is by learning about its anatomy. This includes how it was fashioned, its levels and how God's attributes are reflected within us. This is all part of getting to know your soul. As we go through the following description of your spiritual anatomy, try to take the time to imagine that all this is what is going on inside of you. Just as one can come to a higher awareness of the incredible complexity and brilliance in the design of the human body through learning more about it, so it is with the soul.

The Sages of the Talmud made a relevant statement: "God created the world with ten sayings."[28] This refers to the ten times God declared "Let there be..." in the description of creation at the beginning of the book of Genesis. Even though, on the face of it, these ten sayings refer to different steps in the creation of the world, kabbalistically, they refer to ten filters which dim the light that God pours into creation. Without these filters, there would be no room for human endeavor. God could have created the world with merely one saying, but then, the light would have been too strong, and we would be "washed out." Now, with the light mostly concealed, we are able to serve Him with our own free will.

> *The proper kabbalistic term for these filters is sefiros, related to the Hebrew words saper, to relate, because God "relates to creation" through these filters; sefer, a border, because these filters limit and contain the Infinite Light; mispar, number, because these filters convey God's light in measurable amounts; and even sapir, sapphire, because, like a gemstone, they divide up the one, pure light, allowing us the free will and opportunity to serve God in the world.*

---

28. *Ethics of the Fathers* 5:1

There are ten primary *sefiros* in the kabbalistic chart, known as the Tree of Life. They function like a prism that refracts a single, colorless beam of light into an array of colors. So too, the *sefiros* differentiate and make visible the pure light of God, which would otherwise be too powerful for creation to bear. And just as all the colors that we see become visible only after passing through the prism, yet are contained in unity in their source, so God's endless light contains within it all ten Divine attributes, in potential.

⟿ The Shape of the Body

There are numerous ways that Kabbalists depict these ten *sefiros*. The simplest way is in a straight line, with one *sefirah* following the next in the step-down process of emanation. At times, they are depicted as concentric circles, with the infinite God, the *Ein Sof*, existing beyond all the circles, which become progressively smaller and denser, as the infinite light contracts and weakens it. At other times, God is depicted as being in the center of the circle, and each level of creation is another level in ten surrounding circles. The implication here is that God is at the center of all reality, which "covers Him up," as it were, with increasingly thick layers of reality.

However, the most common method of presenting these forces is the image of a human being. In other words, just as a human being has thoughts, feelings and actions, which can roughly be located in the body as being in the head, the heart and the hands and feet, so God has thoughts, feelings and actions. God's thoughts are His plan and intention for creation; His feelings are His relationship to us—His loving-kindness or His disappointment, at times. And His actions are the way that He runs creation. All of these are attributes of God, ways in which He relates to creation. They are not the essence of God, who transcends any limitations and division.

Nevertheless, by depicting the *sefiros* in this way, Kabbalah is making a statement of what it means to be human, and all the more so, what it means to be created in God's image. For it is not that God's image mirrors mine, but precisely the opposite; a human being, with all aspects of his personality, mirrors God. God's thoughts are pure, His feelings, elevated and His actions, eternal. When a human being aligns his own life according to these deep principles which are conveyed in the Torah, he becomes a true reflection of God. Then he can truly be considered to be created in God's image.

By superimposing the chart of the *sefiros* over the human body, we can arrive at a deep understanding of who we are, how best to use our potential and how to live, in the truest sense.

We will now give a very brief introduction to each of these attributes in order to get a better understanding of how God manifests Himself in the world, as well as to see the attributes that are reflected in the way we as humans have been created. We will refer to this discussion later in this guide, and work to get a better understanding of the more relevant *sefiros*. Keep in mind that all the Divine attributes of the *sefiros* that we are describing in the creation of the world are also living inside of your inner world as a human being created in God's image.

Before we delve into the meaning of the ten *sefiros*, I thought it would be an appropriate time to stop to tune up our spiritual senses so we will be able to "taste the tea" within some of these more abstract concepts.

Overview of
the Ten *Sefiros*

⌁ The Top Three

The first three *sefiros* are Divine forces that might best be called "the vessels of God's thoughts." They are the first stages of the emanation of the world from nothing, and they parallel both abstract and concrete mental process in the human being.

Keser—Crown

Keser is the first of the *sefiros*. It represents the initial Divine impulse to create the world. In the framework of a human being, it expresses itself in the initial act of will that arises in a person's mind, motivating them to action, before even thinking about it. Thus, it is called "crown." For just as a crown sits atop a person's head, and not in it, so the influence of *keser* precedes cognition and our rational senses. It is the part in our thoughts that is unified with the original "endless light" before being broken up by the prism. The position of *keser* being centered on the top of the head also implies its additional connection to the other spheres that are placed in the center below it.

Chochmah—Wisdom

The second of the ten *sefiros* is *chochmah*, which translates as wisdom. It is the first of the "intellectual" *sefiros* and corresponds to the right side of the brain. *Chochmah* represents God's initial concept of creation; God's flash of vision to create a world, before all the details were worked out. In human beings, it manifests itself in abstract ideas. A *chochmah* thought is like a eureka! moment. It is a grasp of an entire idea or concept in its purity, before moving on to be expanded upon and made more concrete.

Binah—Understanding

Binah is located on the upper left side of the chart, and, in human beings, it corresponds to the left side of the brain. It is related to the word *boneh*, to build, for it takes the abstract sparks of *chochmah* and expands upon them, bringing them to a more understandable level. *Binah* is the force to take the building blocks that are provided by *chochmah* and organize them into something functional.

◝ The Virtual Sefirah

Daas—Internalization

Daas, also translated as knowledge, is technically not one of the *sefiros*, but rather, is a new level of awareness that is created through the union of *chochmah* and *binah*. It is a type of integrated knowledge that indicates a deep, intuitive grasp of the subject in question. *Daas* is positioned in the center column of the chart, directly under *keser*, but below the level of *chochmah* and *binah*. It therefore has the benefit of a special relationship to the upper three *sefiros*, to the extent that it is considered the place of *ruach ha-kodesh*, spiritual knowledge, which is a level of understanding that is a tangible reflection of a spark from *keser*. *Daas* is sometimes counted as one of the ten *sefiros*, when *keser* is considered too high to be included.

∼ **The Seven Lower Sefiros**

The seven lower *sefiros* are all located below the head and down to the feet of the image of the body. They are considered to be more emotional and practical attributes. The top three of these seven lower *sefiros* were personified by Abraham, Isaac and Jacob; as we learned about the positive aspects of our three main personalities, we were actually seeing how these *sefiros* manifest themselves in ourselves.

Chessed—Love

Chessed represents God's desire to give gratuitously to creation. When the *sefirah* of *chessed* shines, creation is filled with abundance and blessing. In human beings, it corresponds to the right arm, and is expressed through unconditional giving and acts of kindness. *Chessed* represents expansion and growth without any bounds.

Gevurah—Restraint

The *sefirah* of *gevurah* represents God's strength and power. When God stretches forth His hand to smite His enemies, He is manifesting *gevurah*. When that same power is directed inward, it is manifest in the withholding of goodness and blessing. In a human being, *gevurah* is associated with the left arm and it represents boundaries, restriction and self-control. It is the opposite of *chessed*, yet provides a means for true *chessed* to be expressed, as it harnesses it and directs it in a productive framework. It also represents contraction, with its inward focus, rather than the outward expansion of *chessed*.

Tiferes—Beauty and Balance

The trait of *tiferes* is born out of the healthy balance of *chessed* and *gevurah*. It manifests itself in the amazing balance and harmony of creation. Inwardly, it creates the clarity to experience and act truthfully. *Tiferes* in not merely a combination of *chessed* and *gevurah*, it is a quality of its own that integrates the two, much like *daas* internalizes *chochmah* and *binah*. *Tiferes* is located in the center of the body below *chessed* and *gevurah*, corresponding to the heart.

Netzach and Hod—Dominance and Empathy

Netzach, which means dominance or eternity, is a more physical representation of *chessed*'s expansive quality. (Thus, it sits under *chessed* on the chart of the *sefiros*.) It represents the dynamic force that propels life and creation forward, the thrust of the universe outward from the center. It also represents God's eternal word, which moves through history, influencing and uplifting all of life. On the personal level, *netzach* is expressed through leadership and imposing one's view on the world in a forceful way. One is clear about what one wants to achieve, and strives determinately to execute one's intentions. *Netzach* is associated with the right thigh—the dominant leg, that carries one forward in life.

Hod is located on the left thigh. It represents the passive admission and acceptance of whatever challenge one faces. Rather than taking the offensive, *hod* responds with empathy and strategies to keep peace, while allowing the challenge to pass as quietly as possible.

Yesod—Foundation

Yesod is the final channel through which God's light passes before entering this world. It manifests the perfect balance of expansion and contraction, as expressed in the preceding eight *sefiros*. It lies on the center column of the chart of the *sefiros*, and on the human level, it corresponds to the male reproductive organ, which is the channel through which the very essence of a man flows, in the creation of new life. Just as this organ is the one part of the body that both gives and receives in the same act, so does the attribute of *yesod*. *Yesod* represents the perfect amount of giving, for the total need of the receiver, without sacrificing the sanctity of the giver in any way. Similarly, *yesod* represents the ability to become involved in the positive use of the physical world without being pulled down by negative influences. The stability of its internal spiritual strength is always strong enough to prevent such a falling.

Malchus—Kingship

Malchus is like a vessel that receives the light of all the upper *sefiros* and then humbly shares it with the world. Its function is to reveal the final combination of forces that assembled above. *Malchus* represents kingship, in that it brings all the higher levels down to earth, and allows the world to experience godliness in the physical world. On the human frame, *malchus* is associated with the mouth, which reveals the inner thoughts and feelings of the individual. It is also associated with the feet, which are the parts of the body that touch the earth. *Malchus* expresses total humility in its allowing the content of the preceding *sefiros* to be expressed through it, in the same way that King David was a humble representative of God in this world.

Regardless of which explanation one prefers in understanding what it means to be created in the image of God, one thing that we certainly must acknowledge is that the essence of who we are is immeasurably valuable. Let's see how that plays a role in our lives.

The Obligation
of Self-Esteem

～ Intrinsic Value

If we had no other understanding of the concept of being created in the image of God, the fact that every person bears the inner jewel of the soul is of tremendous consequence. To be created in God's image is a treasure of infinite value—which we all possess and that can never be diminished. And even though there are times in life when you will lose sight of your intrinsic value, you can always work your way back to realizing that "You" are priceless. This is so central to Jewish thought, for the way we live from day to day—with all its emotional and psychological challenges—is profoundly influenced by the clarity with which we are aware of our incredible intrinsic value.

"Pride in the awareness of the greatness and elevation of your soul is not only proper, but is actually an obligation. It is a binding duty to recognize your virtues and to live with this awareness."[29]

Today, low self-esteem plagues millions of people around the world. Countless people go through life imprisoned by their insecurities, lacking reason to believe in themselves. How many wrong choices are made due to a lack of self-esteem, how many

---

29. *Toras Avraham*, p. 49 R. Avraham Grodzinki.

opportunities lost! It seems as though modern society is pushing people to renounce their uniqueness and follow the trends and fashions of the rest of the world. Yet, if people knew of the gold mine within, they would not be so vulnerable and open to society's negative trends.

◠ Love Your Neighbor—Love Yourself

The verse "Love your neighbor as yourself"[30] is a central tenet of the entire Torah. Notice that the verse makes loving others contingent upon loving ourselves. Sadly, people who do not believe in their own essential value will always find it difficult to love others. For how can you trust that someone else loves you if you feel unworthy of love? And how do you give to others if you feel you have nothing valuable to give? Over my years of teaching, I have met couples who seem to be so compatible and have so much to offer their marriages. But when one of the spouses didn't believe in the value of his or her contribution, it ate away at the roots of their love for each other. They never trusted in a valid reason to be loved. Compliments and other expressions of love weren't believed to be sincere. Eventually, their worst nightmare became true. They no longer had a genuine functional relationship to work with, and the marriage ended.

◠ From Within

The Sages of the Talmud asked several questions: "Who is wise? Who is strong? Who is rich?" And they answered: "A wise person is someone who learns from others. A strong person is someone who has self-control. A rich person is someone who is happy with what he has."[31]

---

30. Leviticus 19:18.
31. *Ethics of the Fathers* 4:1.

Notice how these definitions fly in the face of those offered by contemporary society. A wise, strong or rich person is not someone who has amassed a large amount of those items. Rather, it is someone whose wisdom, wealth and strength are internal, and thus cannot be taken away. If our self-esteem is based upon external factors—how much money we have or how attractive we look—our sense of self-worth will be fleeting and flimsy, since none of these things last forever. And even if we were secure in their acquisition, there will always be someone who has more than us, compared to whom we feel inferior.

However, an openness to learn from others, the strength of self-control and a sense of contentment are things that can never be taken away. They are a direct result of our Divine image, which includes our free choice. We choose to be content with what we have, we choose not to follow our lower cravings and we choose to keep an open mind. And even if we fall, the potential to choose again correctly is always with us.

I read of a reputable lecturer who was giving a seminar on self-esteem. He started by holding up a twenty dollar bill and asked, "Who wants the twenty dollars?" Many hands went up. He pushed harder until most of the crowd honestly showed that they wanted the money. Then he dropped the twenty dollar bill on the floor and asked, "Who wants it now?" Of course, most of the people showed they still wanted it. Then he stepped on the money, crushed it into the dirty floor and asked, "Now who wants the twenty dollar bill?" The crowed still showed their hands. The lecturer then made his point. "Ladies and gentlemen, you have just learned a powerful lesson in self-esteem. Even though I dropped the money, stepped on it and crushed it into the floor, it did not lose its value. So too, when you make mistakes and fall and get crushed by the bad choices you make, you will never lose your value in the eye of those who love you."

It sounds so nice and fuzzy. Makes you feel so good. The problem is that it's not true, since what if someone, God forbid, doesn't have anyone who loves them? Does this mean that they are not worthy of self-esteem? The Jewish view is that our worth should not be dependent upon what other people think or feel about us. Our value is intrinsic to being created in the image of God. The gold mine is inside of us regardless of what others see or don't see.

~ **Never Forget Your Worth**

Even after we realize the uniqueness of being human, without conscious review, we will be vulnerable to forgetting it, and thus lose the dignity and the moral expectations that it entails. Keeping the awareness of our true nature at the front of our minds is the ammunition we need on the battlefront of life. Pressure from friends, family and society can push a person to make choices that he would not make otherwise. When your integrity or individuality is being tested, it is the strength of your sense of true self-worth that will provide you with the clarity and strength to succeed. The job of a sports coach is to pump up the confidence of the players: You're the best! You're going to win! You've got it in you! Now go get them! This works for athletes who are willing believe their coach. In real life, though, it's far too easy to fall back into negative patterns of thoughts. How difficult it is to dig for gold in a place where you doubt there is any to be found.

According to the Torah, there is a gold mine in each and every one of us. It is covered up by the many destructive voices that disrupt our clarity. Learning how to recognize and reject these internal and external voices is important for personal growth. Even in difficult situations where you haven't yet developed an authentic sense of self, you can still rely on the knowledge that you are made in the image of God. You can say to yourself, "Even though I've made the wrong choices now, and feel like a loser, I know that it is only because I am out of touch with reality. I am created in God's image. I can choose something different tomorrow. That is the truth; not the illusion that I am feeling right now."

In the early 1980s, I vividly remember when Rav Simcha Wasserman, *z"l*, came to speak to some of the beginners, including me, at Aish HaTorah. At one point he said that in every one of us is a beautiful pearl... Then tears came shooting out of his eyes and he cried. "But the problem is that they are all covered with mud," he continued. I could not believe the incredible love he had for all of us. I was so moved that I felt this need to remove the mud from my own *neshamah* in order to uncover my own pearl and allow it to shine as it should.

One of the biggest weapons used by low self-esteem is the repetition of a self-destructive thought or statement. Something that may have happened in one's childhood could haunt them for the rest of their life. Many people have been the main character of the following story in one form or another.

Ten-year-old Josh Berman is trying to build up his confidence. He joins the local baseball team, with the hope that a little success will bring self-esteem to the rest of his life. Unfortunately, he lacks the natural skills to be the pitcher or take some other infield position, but he gets his share of secondary responsibilities. Somehow, the team makes it to the finals, and in the second half of the final inning, bases are loaded with the other team up to bat. Fortunately, his team is ahead by one point, so all they have to do is catch the ball and Josh's team is the winner. The coach puts our hopeful star out in left field as this game is just about to end. Unfortunately, so is the day, with the sun setting right behind the batter. Sure enough, the ball is hit far out to left field. Without having to move very much, it looks like Josh is going to be a hero. The ball seems to be heading right into his glove, as though it was sent there intentionally to give our little champ a moment of fame, and a lifetime of self-esteem. He lifts up his hands as the ball slams into his glove. As the crowd is screaming, he starts to close his hand around the ball. At that moment, the rays of the setting sun shine from behind his glove and blind him enough to make him lose his bearings. Poor Josh drops the ball. Game over. They lose.

What's all the fuss? So they lost the series—it's just a game. Everyone will understand what happened.

Perhaps, but not to little Josh. "I'm such a jerk," he says to himself. And not just once, but over and over again for years. Josh, now thirty-two years old, has been calling himself a jerk every time he did anything wrong since fifth grade. He hears those words haunting him every time he faces a challenge in his life.

However, every time he says this about himself, he is violating a major principle of Jewish outlook. "Not only is the one who hates his fellow called 'wicked' the one who hates himself also is called 'wicked.'"[32] Josh is limiting his ability to achieve the true purpose for which he came into this world. That is the true tragedy of our little baseball champ.

Many people seem to think that self-destructive talk is okay. People who would never speak an ill word of others find it perfectly acceptable to mentally and verbally abuse themselves. After all, what could be the problem? They are not hurting anyone else. Yet, obviously, they are hurting someone very important, someone to whom they have the greatest responsibility. Just as they have no right to speak negatively about another person who is created in the image of God, they must not speak badly about themselves.

~ Strength from Above

The Jewish perspective of self-esteem extends to another level beyond the awareness of our underlying value as a soul. Our abilities to actualize our individual purpose are also a gift that God gave us. Therefore, once we have figured out what our mission is, we must become aware of the ability we have to actualize our vision of a meaningful life.

---

32. R. Menachem Mendel of Kotzk.

"If you truly believe that God has given you a unique mission in this world, then you should believe He has given you the ability to successfully fulfill it."[33] This means that even while you hear every excuse why you lack the skills to achieve your goal, if you want to do it for the right reasons, God has the ability to use you as His agent to get the job done. (See my song, "Back to Your Soul" at www.realyouproject.com)

When I first went to yeshiva, I was an active participant in the classes and discussions about philosophy. Then it was time to attempt to study Talmud. Not only did I not understand a word of Aramaic, but there was no punctuation to help me figure out where an idea started and ended. I really tried, but acquisition of languages was always a challenge for me, and there were so many concepts that I had never heard of that even when I was told the translation of the words I had no idea what they are talking about. "I guess I am not cut out for this," I remember saying to myself day after day. Then something changed. As I became more aware of a living God running this world, including my life, I decided to just ask Him to help me learn and understand the Talmud. I knew it was what He wanted of me and therefore the ability to succeed was not far away. Everything started coming together, my vocabulary and comprehension of the concepts found their way into my mind. Thank God.

In summary, our self-esteem is deeply connected to our definition of what it means to be a human being. The clearer we are about our intrinsic value—not only in believing in our value but also in our ability to fulfill our mission in this world—the stronger our self-image will be.

_____

33. Rav Tzadik of HaKohen, *Tzidkat Hatzadik*, §154.

Journal

1. What are the negative statements that you hear whenever you make "the same old mistake"?

2. Do you believe that these statements are true?

3. Do you believe that your weakness is evil or just limiting your performance in life?

4. Why is it that this weakness has nothing to do with your intrinsic value?

5. Write a positive statement in response to each of the negative statements you say to yourself.

6. Write the positive statement down on a paper and take it with you wherever you go for the next few days. Read it over and over again until you are sure to remember it. Next time you hear the negative statement, immediately start repeating the positive response.

The Truth Within the Lie

S o we now know that we are created in the image of God. We
have every reason to believe in our potential. We can now
live a spiritually aware life without getting convinced that we are
anything lower than a precious jewel. Right?

It's not that simple. Just as many things we know to be true
fade in and out of our consciousness, so does the awareness that
we are human beings. How could we forget such an essential
part of life? The gold mine inside should be something we watch
carefully and never forget about. Yet we mislead ourselves to even
think we are no less than a relative of the monkey at the zoo.

To understand how we allow ourselves to believe such an
absurdity, let's look at a fascinating statement from the *Zohar*:
"Whoever wishes to successfully lie should use truth as a basis."[34]
In other words, the most misleading lies contain a small dose of
truth. The most effective way to get someone to try a new diet, a
new religion or a new financial scam is to first present the part of
the product that is truly beneficial. Once they have been convinced
of that which is true, they are more likely to grant credibility to
the lie buried within.

---

34. *Zohar* 2:1b.

∼ Life in the War Zone

Perhaps the reason why we allow ourselves to believe that we are little more than advanced monkeys is because our contem-porary society is constantly presenting us with a true point of similarity between ourselves and the great apes. Certainly, from a physical standpoint, there are enough similarities between man and monkeys to suggest a family relationship.

Notice how visitors to the zoo react differently to the monkeys than to all the other animals. People laugh at them when they do silly things, such as eating a banana or swinging on a tire. By themselves, these actions are not so funny. But since the monkeys resemble us so strongly, they become a source of entertainment.

The human soul actually has two main parts: a higher soul, cre-ated in the image of God with its various parts, as well as a lower soul, called the "animal soul" (*nefesh ha-behamis*). These two are in constant warfare.

The animal soul is a spiritual force that is deeply connected to our physical bodies. Its primary concern is the acquisition of food, survival, physical pleasure and other base drives we also find in animals. It is the chief opponent of our power of choice, as it pulls us into instinctive, animalistic behavior. It is this soul that feels an affinity with the monkey in the zoo, and it is this soul that all of secular society is trying to reduce us to. By itself, it is not nec-essarily bad. Properly harnessed, it is an extremely powerful force. However, if misused, it can take us to a level lower than that of animals.

Thus, if it seems at times that the monkey is our next of kin, it is only because we also have an animal soul within us, which we struggle to control. The problem is that in many ways, it is easier to identify with our animal souls than with our Divine image, for doing so does not obligate us to live up to a higher moral standard. Living in the image of God creates obligations that many people choose to avoid.

This deception is part of the design of the world and our challenge of free choice. It can be better understood by looking at an amazing story from the introduction to the *Zohar*.

God looked through all twenty-two letters of the Hebrew alphabet to choose which letter He should begin the Torah with. In a fanciful narrative, each letter (starting from the end of the alphabet) comes before God and presents its virtues, only to be dismissed by God when He finds some fault with it as well. In the course of this story, we learn about the deeper meaning of each letter, hinted to in its name, its shape and its position in the alphabet.

~ Kuf, Sheker, and Emes

When the letter *kuf* makes its appearance, it proudly states that it can be found in the word *kodesh* (קודש), which means "holy." God, however, rejects the letter, because *kuf* is also the middle letter of the word *sheker* (שקר), which means "falsehood," and God cannot start the Torah with something that is associated with a lie.

If we compare the word *sheker* to its opposite, the word *emes* (אמת), which means "truth," we can see how much they differ.

In Hebrew, the word *emes* is composed of three letters—אמת. These are the first, middle and last letter of the Hebrew alphabet, implying a certain stability. That which is true is constant; it remains firm from beginning to end. In addition, each letter of the word *emes* has a firm basis to stand on. The letters *aleph* (א) and *tav* (ת) stand on two "legs," and the letter *mem* (מ) has a horizontal base. This implies that truth is something solid, unwavering, upon which you can rely. Finally, the bottom of all three letters is flush with the line of writing.

The word *sheker*, on the other hand, is the exact opposite. The whole word stands upon only one point—the leg of the letter *kuf* (ק), just as falsehood bases itself on a single point of truth that it has appropriated. Rather than being spread throughout the alphabet, the three letters of *kuf*, *resh* and *shin* are all at the very end of the alphabet, and spell out the word *sheker* when reordered. This suggests a backhanded sort of behavior. Even the letter *kuf* by itself is considered impure. The *Zohar* points out that the leg of the letter *kuf* descends below the writing line, which signifies the soul's descent into the lower desires.

Furthermore, the *kuf* is the middle letter of the word *sheker* (שקר). When we spell out the letter *kuf* in full, we get קוף, which, in Hebrew, means "monkey" (*kof*). This means that the image of the monkey, the *kof-kuf*, is at the middle of the greatest lies that we can tell ourselves—that we are no better than monkeys. That is because the monkey is a powerful example of the point of truth hidden within each lie.

This difference between man and monkey is also alluded to in the differences between the letter *hei* (ה) and the letter *kuf* (ק). Kabbalistically, the letter *hei* represents the human soul, which has five essential parts (*hei* being the fifth letter in the Hebrew alphabet). The Torah says when God created man, "He blew into Adam the breath of life." Indeed, the sound the mouth produces when blowing is that of the letter *hei*. However, if you take the letter *hei* and draw the line on the left side down, it turns the letter into a *kuf*. That is, if a person lets himself be drawn after every lower craving, his soul becomes little better than a monkey's. It's not a coincidence that the most obvious physical difference between a human and a monkey is the latter's tail, which is also the difference between the letters *hei* and *kuf* (ה ק).

Thus, God could not have started the Torah with the letter *kuf*, because it stands for the great lie that human beings are no better than monkeys. Yet, such an assumption is directly opposite the claim of Torah, that we are created in the image of God, and that the Torah is true.

The monkey deceives us into thinking that we are not much different than he. The consequence of such a lie is that it causes us to throw away our human dignity, our essence, our Divine image. What makes us unique is our Divine soul. God breathed life into Adam, and breathes life into every human being—at every instant—since then.

In your daily life you may not hear a voice saying that you are a monkey, but if you *do* hear some of the rationalizations that cause you to forget your dignity and spiritual value—know that in essence they are saying the same thing.

∽ Summary

Although our soul, created in the image of God, has incredible intrinsic value, our animal side works hard to convince us that we are no greater than a lowly monkey. We must make every effort to remember that our physical side is not who we are but is to be utilized by our higher, Divine soul, to help fulfill our dignified purpose in life. It takes an ongoing conscious effort to refresh our minds about what we are and what we are not. Here are some exercises to help.

Journal

R. Simcha Bunim of Peshischa taught that one should have two pockets: in one, a note saying, "I am but dust and ashes,"[35] and in the other, a note saying, "The world was created for me."[36]

The first note tells you not to identify with your animal side, for that is the part that will turn back into dust and ashes when the physical body returns to the earth.

The second note reminds you that your life is considered as valuable as the whole world. This is why saving one person's life is like saving the world. That one person could be you.

Try it. Write two notes and whenever you catch yourself being focused too much on the physical, putting too much emphasis on success, ego and other temporary desires, then it's time to take out the note that says "I am but dust and ashes."

When you are suffering from a feeling of failure, low self-esteem or disconnection from your soul, take out the note that says "The world was created for me."

Does this help?

---

35. Genesis 18:27.
36. *Sanhedrin* 37a.

16

The Five Districts of the Soul

A powerful way to hold onto clear awareness of your soul is by learning more about its anatomy and the character of its different parts. Let's start with an overview.

Just as we saw the physical body reflecting the ten *sefiros*, the body also reflects the levels of the soul. The lower levels correspond to the lower levels of the body—the feet, for instance, which have the least amount of consciousness. After that comes the heart, where we feel things, and the head, which is higher still, incorporating and uplifting everything below it. There are even higher, more hidden levels, of faith and unity.

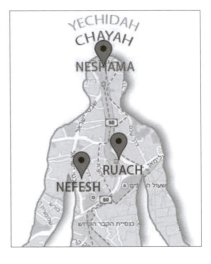

The soul is a spiritual entity; though not a foreign or distant one. Every human being has a soul and can feel it—but not all of it, and not all of the time. This is because the layers of the soul are like a ladder stretching between heaven and earth, connecting us to God. Metaphorically speaking, we can picture the soul as a mountain. The bottom part of the mountain, the broadest area, is that aspect of the soul that all living creatures share. Higher up are the levels unique to human beings. Above that are levels that can even touch the Divine. At each level there are unique sites that should be deeply considered. Ironically, the people who live at the bottom of the mountain have just as much potential for actualizing themselves as the people who make it to the top. Our tour, however, will start at the bottom of the mountain, and we will ascend from there.

∼ Hello Soul

Rather than describe the various districts of the soul theoretically, we will try to actually experience each level as it manifests itself in our lives. The vehicles we will use to ascend this mountain are our bodies, our emotions and our intellects, which together allow us to understand things that might otherwise be too abstract. It is possible to become aware of the spiritual dimension of our lives by learning how to translate the meaningful activity and feelings that we already experience on a regular basis into spiritual terms. This allows us to create a space in our daily lives to form a deeper connection with our souls.

For instance, imagine you go out to dinner with your friends. The restaurant is pleasant and the food is tasty. The waiters place hot garlic bread on the table, with lots of hor d'oeuvres. Finally, they arrive with large plates of your favorite food, which you eagerly devour. An hour or two later, you return home satiated.

Now, let's describe a different scenario: It is the same night and you are in the same restaurant. You are sitting with your friends, waiting for your food, when suddenly, at the next table, a man stands up and starts gesturing wildly. His bulging eyes and blue face indicate that he is choking. His wife and children sitting at the table start screaming in fright. No one knows what to do—except you. You jump up quickly, knocking the hor d'oeuvres all over your clothing, but you don't care. You grab the man from behind, and apply the Heimlich maneuver, which you learned in a first-aid course. After a few thrusts, a large piece of food becomes dislodged from the man's throat, and he throws up. Unpleasant as it is, you are grateful that the man is safe. However, your clothes are a mess, and you no longer have an appetite. You take a rain check on the evening, and return home, still hungry.

But what happens the next day, the next week, or the next year? Which will you remember better—the food that you ate or the man's life that you saved?

Saving the man's life was far from physically satisfying. It may have even been difficult and unpleasant, yet years later, you will still have a "good taste" from it in your mouth. This is because it was a meaningful act that connects directly to your spiritual essence, which is created in the image of God. Physical pleasures are limited, just as physicality itself is limited. They do not go into your spiritual essence and have only a passing effect on your body, which is, in itself, temporary. Spiritual pleasures, however, are un-limited by time, and as a result, can bring satisfaction to the part of you that also transcends physical restrictions.

Becoming aware of the difference between physical and spiri-tual pleasures makes them easier to identify and differentiate, and easier to make conscious decisions. Now, think about the types of pleasures that the consumer based culture around you is tell-ing you to pursue: get rich so you can eat at the best restaurants, enjoy the greatest comforts and satisfy your body to the ultimate degree. Yet such a life, while rich in physical pleasure, may be totally lacking spiritual sustenance. Ironically, you can have ev-erything you want, but still go home "hungry" for what you need. Your decision was based on the culture's need for you to consume and not on your conscious decision of what was right for you.

Imagine that we had everything that the advertisements were pushing us to buy. It would be a life without any lasting mean-ing. It would be delicious and feel good, but we would still feel unsatisfied and hungry for more. Our temporal bodies would be satisfied, but our eternal aspect would still be yearning for more.

There would be nothing to achieve, no one to give to, no kindness to share with the world or the people you love. Most people would feel a tremendous void, since they would be lacking life's most essential spiritual nutrients.

It would be extremely difficult to survive in such a state; yet, that is precisely how many people live their lives. Some people are fortunate enough to find meaningful activity to fill the void. Others escape into the world of digital distractions, with their smartphones, their computers and anything else that gives them temporary pleasure—anything to avoid reality.

We can feel our soul in one of two ways. Either we can hold back, even temporarily, from indulging in some superficial and distracting pleasure, and then feel deeply the sense of emptiness that remains. "Why did I waste so much of my valuable time indulging in emptiness?" This feeling wakes us up to what we are really looking for, which is the fulfillment of the soul.

Try it now. Think back on the most recent time in your life when you felt embarrassed by the amount of time you allowed yourself to waste. Now try to feel the need to make up for it with a stronger spiritual awareness.

On the other hand, we can also feel our soul by recalling those experiences that left a lasting mark on our lives and gave us a feeling of inner happiness. Perhaps it was going out of your way to help a person in need. Or overcoming a difficult challenge that you never dreamed you could face. Or perhaps it was a display of inner strength, in which you denied yourself something very tempting, because you did not want to lower your dignity or spiritual level. Give yourself some time to recall and appreciate these moments of pleasure. If you can do that, then you will surely feel the presence of the soul in your life. It is more present and perceptible than you may have realized. Once you see it and recognize it, it's time to say, *Hello, soul, nice to have you on board.*

Journal

1. List a few things you have done which give you a feeling of spiritual pleasure when you think about them, i.e., saving a life, bringing joy to someone who was in deep pain, setting up a couple who decided to get married.

2. As you think about each of these events, say, *Hello soul!*

_____

_____

_____

_____

_____

_____

_____

_____

_____

_____

_____

_____

_____

_____

_____

⌇ **Take Your Soul on a Date**

When looking for a soul mate, a person experiences their potential spouse on multiple levels. All levels of the soul are active. The lower levels want to see if they are attracted physically and emotionally, while the higher levels want to see if their values and life vision are in sync. Let's follow a dating couple to see the soul in action.

First date: Boy meets Girl. Boy arrives at the hotel lobby first where he waits for what he hopes will be the most beautiful girl he has ever met. Boy's *nefesh* level of the soul gets excited as a beautiful girl walks toward him. Boy's *nefesh* gets a letdown when the girl passes right by him to meet some other guy. Boy's *nefesh* gets a letdown when he sees an unattractive girl walking toward him. Boy's *nefesh* gets excited when she continues to walk by to some other guy. Then Girl approaches him and says, "Are you Boy?" He answers, "Yes, I am." And they fall in love and live happily ever after. I'm sorry, but that only happens in Hollywood, and even Hollywood is wising up to the truth. What really happens goes more like this; Boy's *nefesh* finds Girl kind of attractive except for the really really big wart on the side of her neck. She is still quite attractive but Boy just never pictured himself with a warted neck. "I hope I don't end up liking her," says Boy. But as they actually start to communicate with words and feelings, Girl's warm personality starts to dominate the attention of Boy. Now the date is not limited to the *nefesh*. His *ruach* level of the soul is starting to get involved a little. Although the first date is somewhat superficial, enough warmth is felt to give Boy a sense of more to come.

Boy goes home confused. She seems like a nice girl. She has something special. But what about the big wart on her neck? Even though he is scared of getting too involved, his friends convince him to give it a chance and go out again.

Second date: There she is. And sure enough there's the wart, as big as ever. Then they start to joke a little. They talk about their families and schools and all kinds of stuff that gets the emotional chemistry moving. The more they talk about things that portray their personalities, the more levels of the soul get involved. At one point, later in the date, Boy is fascinated by what seems like some kind of optical illusion. He notices that the wart on Girl's neck has gotten smaller. How did that happen? Well, when the higher level of the soul gets into the picture it actually elevates your perception of the lower level of the soul. When Boy starts to experience Girl on the *ruach* level, the focus of the relationship begins to move more into the realm of emotions.

By the way, Boy must be very careful. While dating, he may be on a spiritual high, but marriage has its ups and downs. In the middle of a serious argument, Girl's wart can suddenly appear to be larger than her head. So don't ignore what your *nefesh* is saying. Physical attraction is important in marriage, just don't let Hollywood tell you what attraction is.

Back to our date. Things are going well for a second date. They are feeling very comfortable with each other and the chemistry seems to be happening.

Third date: Okay, the joking and light shmoozing is nice, but since their goal is to discover if this is who they want to marry, it is time to start getting a little deeper. This is where Boy starts to ask questions about what Girl thinks about this topic and that topic. Beyond the emotional compatibility, he wants to see where her head is at. They want to see a bit of each other's personality. You can have two people who are both brilliant, but when they speak to each other they are on different channels. But in our story, when Boy talks to Girl, they understand each other. They both speak the same intellectual language. This does not mean that they have to be on the same intellectual level, but they connect well in the realm of thought. This is where the *neshamah* level of the soul is getting involved. The more Boy talks about interesting ideas and perspectives on issues, the more he feels a deeper attraction, not only on the *neshamah* level, but the *ruach* and *nefesh* levels are boosted through what is higher than them. By now the wart has almost disappeared in the eyes of our enthusiastic Boy.

Fourth date: The *chayah* level of the soul is considered to be above the mind. It is far more abstract and harder to detect. Boy and Girl start to talk about what is truly important to them. This is not an intellectual exercise; it is a discussion about how they want to live their lives—how they envision raising kids, where to live, what values are of greatest priority, etc. These are ideas that are theoretical to them but still very real issues in any relationship. (You can get a taste of this when working on a project with others—being part of a team and working toward the same goal. Each individual contributes their piece to the puzzle but they are bound together by a common vision, and a bond begins to develop among the participants.)

As Boy and Girl realize that they share a vision and are both hoping to work together to build a home, they are connecting on the *chayah* level. Of course, until they are really married, this sharing can't be fully experienced, but sparks of potential can be tasted as the common vision starts to unravel.

Fifth date: When Boy and Girl get married (okay, maybe not on the fifth date) they both dedicate their lives to coming closer to God as a team. The gates to the *yechidah* level of the soul are open. This oneness, embodied in the holiness of the marriage, is the closest thing to the highest level of the soul.

Now let's take an even closer look.

Nefesh—**Being Alive**

Nefesh is the lowest, most basic level of the soul. The Torah refers to it in several verses, such as, "God said, 'Let the waters teem with swarms of living creatures (*nefesh chayah*)'"[37] and "God said, 'Let the earth bring forth each living soul after its nature.'"[38] Both these verses, as well as other, similar ones, are speaking about the creation of lower life forms: insects, fish and animals. This is because the *nefesh* is the part of the soul that animates all creatures. It is

a spiritual entity that resides in the body and keeps the physical aspect working and alive. It is, as we will see below, the very life-blood of an organism. The Hebrew word *nefesh* means "desire" or "will," and the *nefesh*-soul can be understood as the primary life force of all animate creatures—the "will to live" in all things. It underlies every creature's desire to grow, develop and preserve its own life and the life of its species.

---

37. Genesis 1:20.
38. Genesis 1:24.

In human beings, the *nefesh* is the lowest aspect of the individual soul. It enters a person shortly after birth and "dies" at the end of his life. In the interim, it plays a crucial role in binding the body and the higher soul together. Mystical writings compare the *nefesh* to the wick of a candle. The higher aspects of the soul are like the flame that constantly rises up; so too, these aspects of the soul long to jump off of the material "candle" of the body and return to their source in God. However, were they to do so, the person would immediately die, for that is exactly what death is, the soul leaving the body empty of spiritual life. Therefore, these higher aspects must maintain a connection to the body, which occurs through the *nefesh*-soul.

Often, the *nefesh* is referred to as the *nefesh ha-behamis*—the animal soul, because it is the "brute" part of a person. For it not only enlivens the body, it is the source of all our lower desires and instincts that we share with the animal kingdom. However, that does not mean that the *nefesh ha-behamis* is intrinsically bad. Without the *nefesh*, we could never express our higher spiritual ambitions in this world. We have a *nefesh ha-behamis* desire to procreate, but from this comes our children and all of the opportunity to express love and affection.

A critical part of the battle for spiritual clarity is to know that although we were created in the image of God, we are also the battleground of an internal war. Our Sages teach us that we actually have a split personality. But don't worry about it driving you crazy. It is totally normal—because we all really have two souls. One is a godly soul and the other is an animal soul. Until now we have only been discussing the godly soul and its thirst for meaning, spiritual accomplishment and a connection with its source.

The source of the animal soul is also spiritual but it is closely connected to your body. It wants survival, food, physical pleasure, power—the same drives we see in animals. When you sense a spiritual side to an animal, this is the part you are seeing. For us humans, the animal soul is a very powerful force within us that can take us to the highest spiritual levels if harnessed properly. This is expressed between a husband and wife when they use their intimacy as a means to connect to each other and to God on a deeper level. On the other hand, the animal soul can take us to the lowest spiritual levels, even lower than animals, as much of the world chooses to do.

Using the metaphor of a candle, even when the wick is in place, you still need some sort of fuel to keep the fire burning. Kabbalah explains that the fuel that keeps the flame alive is the practice of the Torah and the commandments. These provide the practical, emotional and intellectual fuel that allows the animal soul to actually support the Divine soul. In other words, the path of Torah does not require us to kill our lower aspects, for that would rob us of the energy we need to function both physically and spiritually. Rather, the Torah takes all of our "lower" inclinations—our desires, our raw emotions, our passions and will to live—and harnesses them in the service of the higher soul. These become the "fuel" that feeds the flame of the higher soul, at the same time as it bestows meaningfulness and true purpose on all our mundane activities. After all, the animal soul is where much of our life is focused, whether we like it or not. If it is harnessed to carry out the wishes of the Divine soul, there is a double benefit. The animal soul is transformed, now becoming the *nefesh chiyunis*, or the "enlivening soul," and the Divine soul, which would otherwise flee from the physical, now dwells in the body and inspires it, precisely because it is receiving sustenance from the body and the *nefesh*.

~ The Blood Is the Life

The *Zohar* (2:94b) explains that though the *nefesh* connects to the physical, it is still very ethereal and much higher than the body. Thus, the connection point must be that part of the body that itself is most "spiritual." Kabbalists identify this with a particular aspect of the blood. A person's blood is the very source of his life, for if it were to stop flowing, a person's body would wither and waste away.

One of the *mitzvos* of the Torah is the prohibition of eating the blood of an animal. Since ancient times, whenever an animal is properly slaughtered for consumption, its meat is salted to make sure that all the blood is removed. The verse says: "You shall not eat the blood of any flesh, for the soul of any flesh is its blood."[39]

The concept of blood being a higher connection applies to human beings too. It is alluded to in the Hebrew word for Man, *adam*, spelled אדם. The first letter of the word, *aleph* (א), represents the Divine soul. It is united with the next two letters, *dam* (דם), which in Hebrew, means "blood." Thus, a human being is a Divine soul that rests upon the body, via the blood. Taking this idea a step further, the Sages teach that there is a small amount of blood in our bodies that is more ethereal than the rest, and that precisely there, body and soul unite.

The most significant explanation of this idea is that of the Arizal.[40] He explains that this *"revi'is* of blood" refers to the highest element of the blood, namely, the "essential life force of the brain," which, in effect, is the interface between the spiritual [Divine soul] and the physical [body]. The Arizal explains that the *nefesh* actually resides in the highest fraction of blood, which is that which sustains the brain, the interface between the physical and spiritual.[41] The nerves, as well as the veins and arteries, are said to contain the most refined fraction of the "blood."[42]

One of the great Kabbalists of the eighteenth century, R. Moshe Chaim Luzzatto, wrote as follows: "The Divine soul is bound to the animal soul, which in turn, is linked to the most

---

39. Leviticus 17:13.

40. *Etz Chaim* 42:1.

41. *Etz Chaim* 20:5, 40:12, 41:1.

42. *Etz Chaim, Shaar HaMochin* 5.

ethereal aspect of the blood. In this manner, the body and the two souls are bound together [in a chain]."[43]

Throughout the Torah, the color red represents insatiable desire and is associated with the animal soul. When the Torah wants to demonstrate Esau's overwhelming desire for physicality, it quotes him as saying, "Let me gulp down some of that red, red stuff," referring to the red lentils that Jacob was cooking. Not only did he eat it voraciously, he willingly sold his eternal birthright for the temporary pleasure. For this reason, the Torah continues on to tell us that Esau was also called Edom, which means "red."[44]

Other Kabbalistic scholars have explained the "ethereal aspect of the blood" as referring not to the blood itself, but to the neural impulses that run through the brain. "The nerves, as well as the veins and arteries, are said to contain the most refined fraction of the blood."[45] Thus, when we say that the "animal soul" depends on this "blood," it means these neurological processes. This further explains why consuming blood is forbidden in Judaism; it is because this neurological activity directly depends on the blood for sustenance.[46] It is interesting to note that animals that experience fear during the slaughtering process release stress hormones that travel from the brain to the rest of the body. In the process of kosher slaughter, the animal's throat is cut quickly with an ultra-sharp knife, immediately cutting off the flow of blood to the brain. The blood is subsequently drained out, both as a result of the slaughter, and through the subsequent salting. As a result, there are little or no stress hormones found in kosher meat. In other words, the nefesh-soul of the animal, which resides in the

---

43. *Derech Hashem* 3:1:1.

44. Genesis 25:30.

45. *Etz Chaim* 20:05, 40:12, 41:1.

46. Aryeh Kaplan, notes to *Derech Hashem*, part 3, note 3, p. 347.

neural impulses in the brain, is nullified during the act of slaughter, and not consumed by human beings afterward.

~ Feeling the Nefesh

It is not too difficult to identify the presence of the *nefesh* within us, because its voice is constantly being heard—from our basic will to survive to our most passionate desires. Whenever you feel your blood pumping through you, in anger or in desire, it is your *nefesh* that has triggered it. (The Sages say that the *nefesh* is mostly concentrated in the left ventricle of the heart, where it is pumped with the blood through the rest of the body.) Some people are so helpless in the face of their *nefesh* that they become destructive or descend to their lowest, most animalistic desires. Others take control, like a rider directing a horse. In that way, they harness the tremendous power inherent in the *nefesh*, to achieve a truly meaningful life. Rather than letting the horse run unbridled, and getting nowhere or being dragged to harmful places, they maintain control and their human dignity. This is done despite having the same desires and drives as animals.

It is not that these desires are bad—animals are not evil in following their basic instincts; however, more is expected from humans. The *nefesh* can be trained to desire spirituality. It is not impossible or difficult. We have all trained our *nefesh ha-behamis* to some extent by learning to eat with utensils and use a bathroom. When it is trained to desire spirituality, it is called the *nefesh ha-chiyunis*, the life-giving soul, since it gives life and energy to Torah and *mitzvos*. The primary way that the *nefesh* is refined and uplifted is by acknowledging and submitting to a higher power—both through the commandments of the Torah and through a sense of our own, higher selves that we must be true to.

Thus, the *nefesh* plays the central role of connecting the soul to the body. It enables us to regard our life in this world as being an amazing spiritual opportunity. It is precisely because our higher, spiritual self has a connection to the physical world that we can use our bodies and desires to elevate our souls. The *nefesh* is a crucial part of a chain that links our physical actions to the highest level of our soul.

In addition, it allows us to draw down spirituality into this world. This is the idea of creating a dwelling place for God in the lower world (*dirah b'tachtonim*). In the same way that God relies upon our actions to manifest His presence in the physical world, so our higher soul uses the *nefesh* as a means to dwell within and direct the body. These two are actually inseparable. God wants us to use our free will to steer the animal soul to do the important work of building Him a dwelling place in this world. Imagine the honor you have been given of creating a dwelling place for God through your daily actions!

Journal

Try to feel your *nefesh* by becoming aware of the following:

1. You are alive, breathing and conscious.
2. This basic life force is located within you.
3. Feel the location of this life force connected to the blood that flows throughout your whole body.
4. Try to isolate the voices within that are calling for more physical pleasures.

Now say, *Hello nefesh!*

_____

_____

_____

_____

_____

18

Ruach—Soul Psychology

Halfway up the spiritual mountain, there is a small chateau. It is a good place to rest and enjoy the view. We have come quite a distance from the *nefesh*-soul, the noise and the tumult of the lower desires are far below us. Up here, the air is cleaner, the breeze is gentle, and the lush smell of flowers fills the air. We are now in the district of the *ruach*, the second lowest level of the soul.

The word, *ruach*, means "wind" or "spirit" and is first found in Genesis 1:2: "And the spirit of God moved over the face of the deep." Within the human being, it is the part of the soul that unites the *nefesh* and the *neshamah*, and binds man to his spiritual source. It is the root of the Hebrew word *ruchniyus*, spirituality, and it is the cause of human feelings and personality traits. It is also the part of the soul which can distinguish between good and evil, and enters a person at adolescence—twelve years old for a girl, and thirteen for a boy—the time when a person's moral sense is first developing. The primary manifestation of *ruach* is in the emotions. Here, too, we see examples of the word used in this form in the Torah. When the patriarch Jacob hears that his son

Joseph is alive, after thinking him dead for twenty-two years, the verse states: "And Jacob's spirit (*ruach*) was revived," meaning that his heart was revived. In another section of the Torah, in the case of a man who suspects his wife of infidelity, the verse says: "And a spirit (*ruach*) of jealousy overcomes him."[47] In both cases, we see that the word *ruach* is connected to the heart and the emotions. Thus, in order to experience the *ruach* level of our soul, we will take a look at how our emotions are most powerfully felt.

Man has an innate love for his Creator. The soul is like a magnet wanting irresistibly to return to its source. At first, this love is expressed through a child's love toward his mother, since she is the most obvious source of his creation and his continued survival since he was born. As our consciousness develops and becomes more independent, we begin to look for love elsewhere. We develop a need to love and to be loved by someone special. This longing for love has shaped the world of music, poetry and all the other art forms, leading people to feel empty if they have not found their true love. "Love" and "loneliness" are among the most commonly used words in the lyrics of countless poems and songs. Without filling this void in our lives, people feel that their lives have not begun. Unfortunately, for many people, this void is not filled even after they find someone to love; and although they should feel more elevated through the relationship, it makes them aware that they are still longing for something even higher. Why do we have such a desperate need for this higher level of love?

Just as God designed the body with great precision, so he designed every level of the soul. We are born with a need for love, which stays with us our entire lives. That lays the foundation for our loving relationship with God. Life begins with a joining, an expression of love between the father and mother, and continues to be expressed and exhibited in the home where the child grows

---

47. Numbers 5:14.

up. This creates the emotional and spiritual framework that is the basis for our relationship with God at a more mature stage in our life. We start to realize that the basic parental relationship is only a preparation for a much deeper one. Deep down, the soul recognizes God as our Creator and the source for everything we have and will ever receive, and, as such, is the only ultimate focus of our love and emotions.

Our independence is critical for living and to give us free will. Yet it is also detrimental, because the illusion of total independence enables us to forget that there is only one source for everything that exists.

The same can be said of marriage. Most people don't realize that marriage is part of a larger scheme that connects us to the ultimate source of life. The restlessness that destroys marriages is often due to the feeling that there is someone else out there who is better. Someone who is "my ultimate love." Yet such expectations create a need that is totally unrealistic and therefore disappointing. There is someone who is your ultimate love, but He is to be brought *into* your marriage with your spouse. We must be careful not to impose a demand on our spouse to fill in more than what is humanly possible. There will always be the love of your Creator and sustainer who gives you everything you need, including your spouse. He wants you to have an amazing marriage because through that, you bring more holiness into your life, and deepen your connection with Him. The *ruach* level of the soul is where all these emotions are manifested. By channeling them properly, we can lift ourselves to a very high spiritual level.

Ask yourself, "What you are truly longing for?" It is a deep question.

Have you ever felt like you had a taste of what you are longing for?

What was different than other times?

Have you ever had such an experience while alone? If so, take some time to recall the feeling.

You can also feel your deep longing for love. Think about the special people in your life who you love the most. Perhaps you can even feel the innate love you have for yourself. This is an experience of *ruach*. Even when love is confused with unhealthy loneliness or desire, it still provides a taste of the true *ruach* within. Even on that lower level, the soul is still calling out for a relationship with the Ultimate Source of life, and the more you elevate those emotions to God, the more they will become pure *ruach*.

It's true that feeling love for the Ultimate Source of life is more difficult than feeling it for another person. Most people do not wake up in the morning feeling passionate about loving God. It is difficult enough to love the flesh and blood person standing in front of us, even when that person has done so much to earn our love and respect. How much more so is it to love God when it isn't always so clear that He is the source of so much good in our lives. Yet, the Torah commands us to love God with all our heart. How can we be commanded to love? Shouldn't it be a spontaneous reaction welling up naturally from our hearts? One possibility is that by contemplating on the logical, intellectual reasons to love God, the real emotional love that is waiting to be expressed will be ignited. We will discuss this further in the section about the *neshamah*-soul.

～ Feeling the Ruach

In order to give you a taste of your *ruach*-soul, I would like to guide you through a short meditation. Not a silent meditation, but an appreciation for the many things that go on in and around us all the time. Though we usually take them for granted, they are actually mind-blowing. If you can "open the windows of your mind" to tune into what is really happening, you will be amazed. So, let's call the following exercise a "guided tour," since one naturally feels love for something that one appreciates and values.

Unfortunately, human nature is such that we tend to overlook the value of things we already have, unless it is given to us anew. That is why wake-up calls are often required to inspire positive change in our lives, as we will discuss. They do not necessarily tell us something we didn't already know, but they remind us of something that we may have forgotten.

In Jewish practice, the daily prayers and blessings offer an opportunity for reawakening to the amazing gifts that we are given each moment of every day. Prayer is called *avodah she'ba-lev*, the service of the heart. It is in the heart that the *ruach*-soul is felt, and the more a person actively works to keep the miracles of life in focus, the more he or she will experience the presence of the *ruach* in their life.

⟿ Ruach Meditation

Sit quietly. Remove the distractions from around you. Close your phone, turn off your computer, sit back and relax. Now, become aware of your heartbeat. Put your hand to your chest, if you need to. Try to quiet your mind of all the regular buzz of activity. Much of the static in your mind just distracts you from some of the amazing things that are in your life.

Listen to the sounds around you. The cars outside, the air conditioner, the sound of someone in the next room speaking. All these things are producing sound waves that carry messages through the air, to a vibrating sensor in your ears. You not only pick them up, but have the built-in mechanism to translate those signals into logical messages.

Now, reflect on your own mind, which serves as the communication center that sends and receives messages to and from all your main limbs at every moment, down to the micro level of every cell. And far below the level that we can feel or perceive, strands of DNA are constantly delivering their encoded messages to different parts of the micro-laboratories that are embedded in our every cell. Now listen to the message of the journal from Cambridge University that speaks about this:

> *A bacterium is far more complex than any inanimate system known to man. There is not a laboratory in the world which can compete with the biochemical activity of the smallest living organism. One cell is more complicated than the largest computer that man has ever made.*
>
> Sir James Gray

This awesomely complex system is working full time in your own body, and in the bodies of billions of people around the world. Can you imagine what it would be like if the entire world could communicate with the same harmony and cooperation that the parts of our bodies do?

~ The Voice of Soul Demanding Ethical Standards

Another way to experience your *ruach*-soul is by identifying the absolute moral principles at the core of your life. What do you believe is absolutely wrong—not because of your upbringing, or because society says so, but because you know that it is wrong, no matter what anyone says. Take murder, for example. Unless you know that murder is wrong, why not kill someone? It's the easiest way to get something from them that you want. There must be a voice inside us somewhere that tells us that "murder is a crime; don't do it!" Even people who have never heard of the Ten Commandments still know that murder is wrong. Why?

The answer is that our souls know that it is wrong. It is a part of our spiritual essence and a product of our being created in the image of God. Some people will try to reject this by claiming morality is merely a result of social conditioning; that there really is no objective right or wrong (and thus, living like an animal is justified and acceptable). However, if you probe deep enough, you will eventually find that, if they are honest, there is always an absolute truth they hold to be true, and not merely a relative value. Let's illustrate this with an extreme example.

> *It was Nazis who shoved sand down a boy's throat until he died, who tossed candies to Jewish children as they sank to their deaths in a sand pit, who threw babies from a hospital window and competed to see how many of those "little Jews" could be caught on a bayonet, who injected a cement-like fluid into women's uteruses to see what would happen, who stomped a pregnant woman to death, who once snatched a woman's baby from her arms and, in the words of a witness, "tore him as one would tear a rag."*

(*Leonard Pitts Jr., Seattle Times, August 19, 2009*)

There isn't a single person with an ounce of sanity who would claim that these acts were ethical. Everyone would agree they are abnormally cruel and evil acts. Even if someone was insane enough to think that it was morally acceptable to ethnically cleanse the world of Jews, where is there room to consider injecting women with cement? There comes a point where even the greatest heretic will find himself making absolute moral claims, and will have to rely on the undeniable existence of a soul that guides us.

As for your own *ruach*-soul, did you feel it awaken momentarily when you read about the Nazis' crimes above? Were you morally outraged by their behavior? Could you hear the inner voice that tells you that, no matter what, their actions were absolutely evil. If so, that is the voice of your soul. It is the part of you that cares about our elevated status as human beings, with the responsibility to live in this world according to a higher moral standard. Ironically, some of the leading spokesmen for moral relativity claim that it is immoral to refer to anything as immoral. It seems that they, too, are picking and choosing what they want to postulate as ultimate truths, with their desires shaping their thinking.

However, we need not cite such extreme examples to identify our *ruach*-soul. Our souls have an inner recognition of a broad range of subtle principles of right and wrong, though it may require some inner excavation to raise them to conscious awareness. For example, is stealing acceptable? When the Ten Commandments state: "Thou shalt not steal," it is speaking about stealing human beings, such as for slave trade. Most people would agree with that. But what about the more indefinable case of borrowing someone's pen without asking? Is that stealing? I may return the pen, but I probably will not return the ink. Did I steal it? Perhaps it's okay to use someone's ink, since the owner isn't overly possessive of it, or its value is relatively small. What about downloading copyright material from the internet? Is that stealing? Deep down, our souls know the answers to even these scenarios. However, we may have lost sight of the truth, to the point that we need our Torah to provide us with the principles to be applied to these types of cases. The Talmud refers to this inner awareness of ethical principles when it states that an angel teaches the entire Torah to the fetus in the womb. In other words, knowledge of the Torah is part of the very fabric of our being. Even though we are made to forget it upon birth, it is still there, buried inside, making life a process of relearning, rather than learning from scratch. This is the type of reminder I was referring to. When we recognize the truth of a moral principle, we are actually reawakening the awareness we had in the womb. We are recalling what we were once taught, that which has remained deeply planted in our souls. It is the *ruach* level of the soul that identifies with the many meaningful feelings and principles that we base so much of our lives upon. By listening to those inner voices and bringing them more to our conscious awareness, we become connected more to the *ruach* level of our souls.

Journal

To try to feel the *ruach* level of your soul think about the following:

1. Think for a few minutes about the people you love the most.

2. What is this feeling of love and where inside do you feel it?

3. Is it a physical location, spiritual location, or both?

4. Think about some of the values that you are passionate about, i.e., justice, equality, Jewish education, fighting anti-Semitism, etc.

5. Try to find where these feeling are found within you.

Now say, *Hello ruach!*

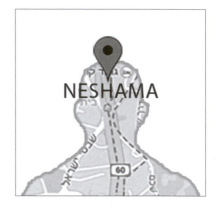

Neshamah—All in the Mind

Moving further up the mountain, we find ourselves near the top. Here, the sun is bright and the air is crisp, and our thoughts become crystal clear. We are now in the third district of the soul, called the *neshamah*, which is the highest level of the soul that resides within the body. The word *neshamah* is from the Hebrew word, *neshimah*, which means "breath." This aspect of the soul is first alluded to in Genesis (2:7), "And the Lord God formed man of the dust of the earth, and breathed into his nostrils the breath of life—*nishmat chaim*." The *Zohar* (3:123b) comments on this verse that God "breathed from deep within Himself," when he gave Adam life. In other words, this level of our soul is something Divine, a breath of God that is at the very heart of our existence. It is a spiritual potential that is specific to human beings and raises us far above the level of the animals, allowing us to develop our higher nature and direct it toward that which is godly. It is the eternal part of the soul, which lives on after we die. Kabbalistic works identify the *neshamah* as an actual portion of the Divine, called a *chelek Eloka mi-ma'al* (Job 31:2), that is within us. Thus, we can envision the *neshamah* as that part of us that is always spiritually connected, which we would call our higher self.

If the *nefesh*-soul corresponded to our actions, and the *ruach* to our emotions, then the *neshamah* is deeply connected to our intellect. If the *neshamah* was visible, you would see it as energy flowing through the brain. In other words, the "seat" of the *neshamah* is in our brains, and it manifests itself through the proper use of our intellects. Indeed, at times it is called the "intellectual soul" (*nefesh sichlis*).

As we have seen, according to the Jewish view, the "Land of the Soul" is far from a settled place. It is a country rife with battles and warring factions, and our job is to learn how to defeat a host of enemies that threaten us. The principle internal battle that wages within each individual is between the *neshamah* and the unrefined *nefesh*, or animal soul. In this struggle, the Animal Soul is constantly trying to overcome the *neshamah* and drag it down to its level. That would mean that the mind, rather than contemplating inspiring truths, such as Torah, spirituality or God, falls under the sway of lower desires, and devotes its energy to justifying immorality.

The opposite of this is when the *neshamah* conquers the *nefesh*. That is, instead of being pulled down into intellectualizing and justifying lower actions, it uplifts the animal soul, and redirects all its passion and drive toward a higher calling—to self-refinement, prayer and Torah study. Note that the primary battlefield is the level of the *ruach*, the emotional soul. Both the *nefesh* and the *neshamah* fight for control of the *ruach*—for human emotions. The animal soul wants to pull a person down by exciting him over the wrong things, and the intellectual soul wants to uplift the *ruach*, and the *nefesh* with it, so that they are motivated and committed to serving God.

Thus, although the essence of the *neshamah* is pure and godly, our work is to differentiate between holy thoughts and unholy thoughts; between thoughts that lift us to God, and those that are nothing more than justifications for improper behavior. For once a thought has entered our minds it travels quickly to the heart. If it is a spiritually healthy thought, we must open our hearts to it and become inspired. This blending of the mind and the heart is crucial for a person to feel alive and motivated, with a sense of meaning and joy. However, a person's thoughts and imagination can just as easily grab hold of destructive thoughts. If these are not quickly blocked, they will descend to the heart where the animal soul will take control. It will then arouse and magnify the desire, until it becomes manifest in inappropriate behavior and actions. It's interesting to note that another possible Hebrew root for the word *neshamah* is *shumah* (שומה), which means to estimate or evaluation. This is because it is the role of the *neshamah* to evaluate every thought and emotion that arises in the mind, and to weigh its validity in a life directed to self-development and spiritual growth.

⮜ Feeling the *Neshamah*

When we use our minds to contemplate holy ideas, we are engaging the *neshamah* in the most direct way possible. Particularly, we nourish the *neshamah* by engaging in the study of Torah. There is no surer way to experience such a high level of the soul. When our thoughts are filled with Torah, our minds and *neshamah* rise to levels unreachable through the performance of any of the other commandments.

People sometimes criticize Talmud study because it seems to over-emphasize hair-splitting details. Page after Talmudic page deal with the minute details of Jewish law. Who really cares if someone's cow gored someone's sheep in a public domain, or one person finds someone else's *tallis* in the marketplace? Yet yeshiva students pore over these texts and debate them endlessly. The reason is that these texts, with all their details, embody God's laws for life, which extend down to the smallest detail of creation.

When we fill our minds with this holiness, we give our *neshamos* a tremendous boost of spiritual nourishment.

If you have experienced the spiritual high of intense Torah study, then you have experienced something of your *neshamah*, and you will understand why this type of study is different from any other, even the most philosophical investigations. Torah study engenders a connection with God that is extremely pure and powerful. If you have not yet experienced such study, you can start with the book you have in your hand right now. In these pages, we have been discussing many concepts of Torah that hopefully have been filling your mind with ideas to think about, all of which relate to who you are and what you are. Of course, this is just the beginning. Each concept discussed here is of infinite depth. However, whatever level of intellectual pleasure you experience is a sign that you are tapping into the *neshamah* level of your soul.

Journal

1. If someone tried to convince you that there was no such thing as gravity how would you feel?

2. What would you think if someone tried to convince you that the Holocaust never happened?

3. Where within you would you be struggling to stop such absurd claims?

4. Try to find more examples of ideas about which you are a hundred percent sure.

5. Use your conviction in these examples to get in touch with your love for truth.

6. If this doesn't help, try getting in a philosophical debate with someone and watch your level of involvement.

Then say, *Hello neshamah!*

_____

_____

_____

_____

_____

_____

_____

_____

_____

_____

20

Chayah and *Yechidah*—
Above the Clouds

⤳ The District of *Chayah*

Looking further up the slope, we see the cloud-covered peak
of the mountain. There, too, we can discern yet another district of
the soul. Yet, it is so obscured that it may not be resting upon the
mountain at all; indeed, it may exist somewhere above it. A closer
look reveals that there are no paths leading up to this next level.
Meaning to say, it is not something that we can directly experience or grasp. Yet, it exists, and has an influence upon us.

This is the district of the *chayah*, the living essence. The *chayah*
is one of the two "surrounding" aspects of the soul; that is, it is
not contained within our bodies, and is thus inaccessible to our
conscious awareness. In general, each level of the soul starts from
a place beyond the body, and only enters into it when the person
is ready. However, the *chayah*, and all the more so, the *yechidah*,
never enter the body due to their rarified nature. Thus, because
it is located outside, the *chayah* is far more difficult to relate to,
describe and experience. There is something about it that is too
abstract for the mind to comprehend (otherwise it would be con-
tainable within the space of the body).

Kabbalistically, the *chayah* is the aspect of the soul that gives
one the consciousness of the Divine life force. It corresponds to
the ideal and primordial, blissful state of Adam and Eve before the

133

sin. Even though it is not directly perceivable, it does influence us on the level of our highest wills and desires. Whenever we have a moment of spiritual inspiration, or the sudden desire to improve ourselves and come closer to God and truth; whenever we have what is called a "peak experience," we are experiencing the influence of the *chayah* in our lives. In those moments, we feel connected to something "higher" than our daily concerns; even higher than our most engaged intellectual endeavors, such as Torah study.

～ Experiencing the *Chayah*

In order to get some small taste of the *chayah*, we must keep an important kabbalistic principal in mind. Much like cells of the physical body contain strands of DNA in which are encoded a person's entire genetic makeup, so does each level of the soul contain some element of the other four levels. Thus, even if we can't reach the level of consciously experiencing our *chayah*, we can find reflections of it within our understanding.

When I was in college, there were times when I wanted to just leave everything around me. The demands of being a music composer with its complex "religion" of artistic and social expectation were far too superficial to allow myself to become too immersed in them. One of the things I used to do was take a stroll down my street to a park that had a small ditch wide enough for me to lie down and feel as if I was just a small part of the ground—the grass, the earth and almost nothing left of me. I felt so relaxed and free. The less of myself I felt, the more I felt I was part of something much bigger. This became a regular practice of mine. I had no idea what I was enjoying about it until years later when I realized that I was trying to experience the *chayah* level of my soul and its pure connection to God.

In more kabbalistic terms, when you lift yourself to surrender to your true life source, when you humbly recognize and accept that there are some truths that are "higher" than you, so that you annul your own actions (*nefesh*), feelings (*ruach*), and understanding (*neshamah*) to that higher truth, you are experiencing your *chayah*. We will be digging deeper into this idea later.

On a lower level, people get a taste of *chayah* when they work with other people, as a team, for the sake of a higher cause. When everyone feels that they are part of a team working toward something they all believe in—perhaps a humanitarian cause or even a business project—there is a humbling effect of seeing one's small contribution as part of a bigger picture; that is an experience of the *chayah*-soul.

Try to think of a time when you found great energy and inspiration in working toward a goal that you believed in, which transcended your own interests—whether you worked alone, or with others. Where did all that energy come from? While this may not be the *chayah* itself, it does give us a strong sense of it.

∼ The District of the *Yechidah*

Somewhere above the clouds, above the mountain itself, is the fifth district of the soul, called the *yechidah*. Like the *chayah*, the *yechidah* is a *makif*, a portion of the soul that surrounds the body, being too expansive and pure to enter the body itself. The word *yechidah* is from the Hebrew root *yachad* and *echad*, which mean "one and unique." In this case, it signifies the soul's unique essence or unity. It is our union with the source of all life and being; that is, to God. Had Adam stood the test of not eating from the Tree of Knowledge, he would have risen to the level of *yechidah* and experienced a complete unity with God.

Because the *yechidah* is so lofty and abstract, we are mostly unable to feel its direct influence on our lives. Indeed, very few travelers have ever made it to that level and returned, though the rare few that have, have brought us back reports. What they tell us is that they experienced a total oneness with our Creator. The reality of God that they experienced was so intense that they could see it in everything. This is what we testify to when we recite the

Shema: Hear, O Israel, the Lord is our God, the Lord is One. This is not a statement whose meaning we can grasp consciously; though on the subtle, innermost level of our *yechidah,* we can perhaps have some intuition of its meaning. Indeed, one of the amazing things about the prayers of the Torah and the Sages is their ability to connect us with spiritual experiences that we would not be able to figure out on our own.

Journal

The best way to touch your *yechidah* is simply to close your eyes and say: *Shema Yisrael Adonai Eloheinu Adonai Echad.*

⟶ Conclusion

Developing a sense of our own souls enables us to connect to God by having a taste of the godliness that is within us. However, as we have seen, this Divinity is not just a single spark of bright light glowing inside; it is composed of various colors and shades that reflect the way God operates in the world. Each part of the soul is related to combinations of *sefiros* and to upper worlds that Kabbalah speaks about in depth. To truly study and understand the soul would take more than a lifetime, for there are elements of the soul that we will not even begin to touch until after we have passed beyond this world. Still, as travelers on the path to self-knowledge, we have already visited some of the major sites in the Land of the Soul. And there is still much more to see!

21

Back Down to Earth

✎ Easy Paths to Spiritual Growth

Experiencing the soul can be quite intimidating after learning about the complexity of its levels and attributes. But in truth there is no need to feel afraid of the challenge of feeling the soul, because although understanding the soul is the most direct path to spiritual awareness, there are easier paths that can be helpful to climb to a higher level as well. These are the life experiences that naturally wake us up to a stronger connection to our soul and purpose in life.

We have all heard of people who made sudden and dramatic changes in their lives. What exactly happened? Was it the result of a sudden insight into life, or the final stage of a slow-brewing process that suddenly rose to the surface?

The truth is, all of us are changing and growing constantly. That is a part of life. Who we are in our teens will not be who we are in our golden years. If we can take note of the successes and mistakes of others, of their inner drives that accelerate their growth process beyond the rate of most other people, we may be able to save ourselves years of struggle and fruitless searching.

I believe that we all can be inspired to change through a wide range of positive influences. For some, it may entail seeing others who have lifted themselves from the lowest to the highest level of accomplishment. For others, it may be a taste of their own first steps toward success, which reveals to them how much they could achieve, if only they applied themselves.

Ask yourself when your personal success inspired you to make a positive change in your life. Did you ever make a difficult sacrifice for the sake of an inner voice of truth or moral integrity? Try to recall something in your life that gave you a powerful surge of energy and incentive to make a big step forward. For some it may have been triggered by taking an inspirational trip to Israel. For others a hike through nature, or even a single inspirational book, could have been enough to push the right inspirational buttons. If we open our eyes, we can learn to perceive the numerous positive miracles that surround us all the time.

Our lives are filled with positive messages and events that can radically change us for the better—if we could only open our eyes to see them, and silence the voice of our inner cynic, which demeans these things as commonplace and ordinary. The birth of a child, for instance, is a positive experience that can wake a person up to life, no less than a near-death experience. The sight of a new life entering the world is almost too amazing to be true, as anyone who has witnessed it can testify. Yet, according to the Torah, this process is repeated in each person's life, every single day. When a person goes to sleep at night, his soul rises up and is deposited in the care of his Creator, who returns it each morning, renewed and refreshed. Every morning, a person experiences a complete rebirth. If we did not take this for granted, we would feel tremendous change and inspiration from the simple act of rising in the morning. The very fact that we wake up is a sign that God believes in us, and that we can accomplish our goals in life.

Journal

1. List a few times in your life when you made great positive change.

2. What event took place before that may have helped inspire you to grow?

_____

_____

_____

_____

_____

_____

_____

_____

_____

_____

_____

_____

_____

_____

_____

_____

~ Inspiration through Role Models

Seeing is believing, especially when trying to make positive change. We could discuss the acquisition of positive traits forever, but when you meet someone who exemplifies a quality that you admire, it makes it so much easier to imagine being able to achieve what you are here to accomplish. For most of us, our role models begin with our parents and older siblings. As we become more independent, rabbis, teachers, mentors and close friends can also serve as powerful sources of inspiration for positive change. Even people we have never met who have achieved something heroic can reach the inner voice of awareness of our potential.

Try to find some examples in your life of people who have served as role models of inspiration. Notice which ones play an educational or mentor role and which are simply inspirational in who they are or what they have achieved.

We cannot just wait for a spiritual role model or guide to appear in our life. It is well-worth the time and effort to find someone who has the experience and wisdom to reach a place of accomplishment that you dream to achieve. As the Mishnah states: "Make yourself a Rav and acquire for yourself a friend."[48] These are two examples of positive influences that we are to actively pursue, learning so many lessons of what to do and what to avoid, making your journey so much smoother.

---

48. *Ethics of the Fathers* 1:6.

Journal

1. Who are your role models?
2. Are you being inspired to grow in a positive way from them?

_____

_____

_____

_____

_____

_____

_____

_____

_____

_____

_____

_____

_____

_____

_____

_____

_____

_____

⌁ **Inspiration through Disappointment**

Sometimes, while heading down a path to our dreams, we are granted a fleeting vision of what we might eventually attain. At the moment that our drive for success dominates our thoughts, we lift up our heads and look down to the end of the path we are traveling, where we may see that something isn't quite right. This is not due to any complex calculations of gains or losses; rather, it is a gut feeling that tells us that our sought-after destination and our true sense of happiness are sadly mismatched.

We are often surrounded by valuable lessons that should serve to inspire us to make positive changes in our life. Sometimes, the messages bear positive inspiration. At other times, we learn from their opposite. But tif we are not ready to lift our heads up to see what is in front of us, we just won't notice either one. Thus, the first step is to make a more active effort to look around us and evaluate what we see. The obvious answers may be staring at us right in the eye.

Almost a Winner

As a young man, my life was totally devoted to music; a world of numerous rules and restrictions that define you as a genuine artist or a commercial cash-cow. Although I was working hard to make it big in the commercial music business, I struggled to maintain my artistic integrity. Indeed, there were only a handful of commercially successful musicians whom I considered my idols. Not only was their talent unbelievable, they admitted to no artistic compromise on the path to commercial success.

I had been recording an album in Los Angeles with one of Hollywood's most talented producer/arrangers: Gene Page. Gene had won numerous Grammy awards for his work with other artists and was once again nominated for the upcoming Grammys. That year, though, Gene could not attend, and so he asked if I could go on his behalf and accept it. Although it seemed a dream come true, I was terrified at the thought of having to stand up in front of millions of people the world over and make a thank-you speech without fainting.

Luckily for me, Gene did not win that year. However, as his delegate, I was treated like royalty; driven in a private limo, and invited to the party afterward for all the music business insiders. After making my way through all the celebrities and glamorous people who I didn't really respect, I was amazed to find one of my idols sitting at a table right in front of me. I was given a front-seat view of someone whom I dreamed to be like. It was a crystal clear picture of what my own life might one day be, after I would make it big.

How disappointing it was for me, then, to see my idol looking so unhappy. Gods weren't supposed to be unhappy! I will never forget the feeling I had of seeing my life's dreams shatter in front of me, and the internal decision I made at that point not to pursue that path any further. Not that I suddenly had some alternative plan for my life. I simply knew there was something wrong, and that if my idol was so unhappy, then I needed to change my own life—if I did not want to become a miserable success.

This was a pivotal transition in my life, which motivated me to make major changes in my plans. I had been so immersed in my previous dreams that it took a shocking image to wake me up.

Journal

1. Think about the greatest letdown you have ever had.
2. Was the thing you were hoping for realistic?
3. Did you define yourself too much by your success?
4. How have your changed since this disappointment?
5. Can you use this disappointment to grow further?

_____

_____

_____

_____

_____

_____

_____

_____

_____

_____

_____

_____

_____

_____

_____

_____

∽ Finding Inspiration in Failure

Although we strive to live our lives in a way that is growth-oriented and meaningful, some of the greatest accomplishments begin precisely when we are at our lowest spiritual level. This is a deep principle latent in the very way the world was designed. "And it was evening, and it was morning, one day."[49] That is, sometimes light only shines when it is preceded by darkness.

One of many examples is in the way a fruit tree grows. We take a healthy seed and plant it in the ground, where it rots until the point of disintegration. Yet, precisely when it reaches its "lowest" state does it sprout forth and grow toward its ultimate potential as a tree. Sometimes, the clearest vision of who we want to be begins to shine when we have fallen the furthest from it. When you have reached rock-bottom and there is nowhere to go but up, a tremendously clear picture of who you really want to be naturally appears; one that you could not see before. Thus, while no one should throw themselves down into such dangerous territory, it would be a shame not to take advantage of the incredible opportunity that moments of despair offer us on the rebound.

I have to share a wild experience that happened on that trip to L.A. when I was sixteen years young. My friend and I became buddies with a great guitar player named Blood. Really nice guy. Lived in a bit of dangerous neighborhood (I believe it was Watts), but he promised that he was going to protect us... and he did. So we moved into Blood's nice well-kept house and everything was great. I even got to meet his father who was a priest. I remember his father asking, "Are you Jewish?" Although I was a little scared of the repercussions, I said, "Yes." He was so excited to meet one of the "Chosen People." I vividly remember

---

49. Genesis 1:5.

him saying, "Now if you were ridin' on a white donkey, I would say that you was the Massiah but since you ain't riding on a white donkey I guess you ain't the Massiah."

Anyway, for some unknown reason, the conditions of Blood's house started to deteriorate and it became very uncomfortable to stay there. You see, Blood had five dogs. Spotty, Rover, Browny, Blacky and, of course, David. I had never met a dog with the same name as me. That wasn't the problem. For some reason, Blood no longer felt it was necessary to take his dogs out of the house to use the bathroom. Rather, he allowed them to "go" wherever they wanted. On the couch, floor, blankets that we slept on... We couldn't take it. We had to find somewhere else to move to. But as we looked in the listings for apartment rentals, the only affordable ones were tiny and covered with cockroaches. Then from the depths of the mud we thought we were stuck in, a wild thought came to my mind. If we wanted a good deal on nice accommodations, the only place to look is where people have so much money that any rent we could offer would be too little to care about. We headed to Beverly Hills. Sunset Blvd. The first mansion, no luck, second, no luck... the third, a woman answers the door.

"Yes, how can I help you?"

"We are here from Toronto trying to sell our music and we wondering if you had a guest house that perhaps you would let us stay in."

"We have a guest house, when would you like to move in?"

"What about tomorrow?"

"Okay. But don't you want to see it first?"

So she walked us through her beautiful mansion and out to the backyard where there was a charming guest house with a swimming pool on one side and a tennis court on the other. And of course a piano.

"Sure, this should do just fine."

And that was it. No rent either. About a month later the owners had a divorce and they needed us to take care of their whole property. Quite a jump from the conditions of Blood's apartment.

When you are in the midst of the lowest points in your life, you can use that as a springboard to places higher than you ever imagined.

When we are looking for something in the dark, a little candle can illuminate an entire room, though the same candle by day is hardly noticeable. So, too, when we try to discover the inner parts of ourselves that are often buried in darkness, we shouldn't give up too easily. We should appreciate the darkness, for it is the setting that helps the light be so much more effective and clear. Even a small insight or illumination can shed great light on our knowledge of ourselves and help us move forward, precisely because we find it the darkness and confusion of unclear self-knowledge!

> *Light a candle in the night*
> *It's a festival of beautiful light*
> *It's a time to see the miracles everywhere*
> *In everyday life*[50]

---

50. From my song, "Candle in the Night."

Journal

Try to think of the lowest point in your life. Did this have an effect on your life choices? If so how? Try to use this as an example to get the most out of every time you have a low point in your life in the future.

_____

_____

_____

_____

_____

_____

_____

_____

_____

_____

_____

_____

_____

_____

_____

_____

_____

∽ **If Not Now, When?**

One day, many years from now, you will reach the last years of your life. You will sit back and review your life with a tremendous sense of joy and accomplishment, with a deep sense of satisfaction, knowing that you made the right choices and achieved all that you were brought into this world to do. You will be ready to face your Creator and move on to the next world with your soul enriched by all the spiritually meaningful achievements of your life.

But what if your backward glance will not be so sweet? What if, like many people, you will be carrying a sense of regret and frustration for a life filled with mistakes and blunders? *How in the world did I mess up my life*, you might wonder. *How did I miss out on such important parts of living?* No one looks forward to hearing such negative voices haunting them in their old age, yet for many people, it seems very difficult to prevent.

The simplest way is to ask yourself those questions *now*. Realizing that there will one day be a final reckoning can inspire a person with the strength and insight to make the best choices possible now. Ask yourself what would make you proud. What do you not want to be ashamed of? What are your priorities and is your life designed to live according to them? If you don't make positive changes by making the right choices, no one else will. If not today, then when?

"Hillel used to say: If I am not for myself who will be for me? Yet, if I am for myself only, what am I? And if not now, when?"[51]

---

51. *Ethics of the Fathers* 1:14.

Journal

Try to imagine your life continuing along the path you are on now. Where do you envision this path will take you? Try to imagine as full a picture as possible.

1. Is there anything about this picture that you don't like?

2. If so, what can you do now to prevent it from happening?

_____

_____

_____

_____

_____

_____

_____

_____

_____

_____

_____

_____

_____

_____

⟿ Tragedy and Near-Death Experiences

Tragedy, too, can serve as a powerful wake-up call to change the way we look at life. Why does tragedy—such as the loss of a loved one—make such a difference in how we view life? We all know that one day, we will reach the end of our lives; did the event of someone else's death teach us something that we were unaware of before?

The answer is that there are different types of knowing. At a funeral, besides confronting human mortality, we also become aware of the duality of body and soul. As we watch the physical body, devoid of all life, being lowered into the grave, the stark contrast between body and soul hits us in the face. What happened to all the physical pleasures that this person enjoyed during his or her life? We realize that nothing of them remains. At the same time, we sense that something eternal does exist—the spiritual acts of prayer, study and kindness that the person did during their life is certainly not lost. In fact, burying the body does not bury the soul; it frees it from its physical confinement, so that it can now enjoy the reward for all the good deeds it did while alive. Unlike the pleasures of the body, the pleasure of the soul is eternal. They make an eternal impression upon one's essential being—the real you—which you take with you.

It's not that we were unaware of our soul before the funeral, but that we simply lost our awareness of what we already knew deep inside. Attending a funeral helps us re-identify with the essential person—the eternal soul—rather than the physical body that will now rot in the ground, at least until the next time we are faced with a strong enough temptation to make us forget what we witnessed.

Thinking about our mortality is not fun; it demands that we take our life seriously. But it has the profound benefit of letting us take real responsibility for our own lives, since we can never know when our turn arrives to join our loved one at the end of the line.

Journal

1. What was the tragedy closest to your life?

2. How did you think differently right after it happened?

3. Are those post-tragedy thoughts still true and relevant to your life?

4. If they have drifted from your awareness, try to remind yourself of these messages.

⌒ **When It's Your Own Life**

An even more powerful wake-up call happens when we ourselves come face-to-face with a life-threatening sickness or accident. For example, if someone is in a car accident and trapped in a way that they cannot escape, you can be sure that until the rescue team arrives, their entire thoughts will be focused upon the people they love and other meaningful issues in their lives. A minute before the accident they were complaining about a stain on their shirt; a minute later, they were doing a major reordering of their values in life. The powerful impact of the event woke them up. If they are lucky, they will hold onto that inspiration and, afterward, re-evaluate their lives for what is truly important.

About fifteen years ago, a radiologist told me that I had a brain tumor. He did not yet know if it was cancerous or not, and I had to undergo a series of MRIs and other tests to discern what was really happening. From that moment on, my life was dramatically different from what it had been moments before. Life had instantly become a small yet precious moment on this beautiful planet, with far too much to achieve in the short time allocated for it. Realizing that my life might be cut short, I understood that my true goals were those of quality and not quantity. Those who I loved became even dearer to me. The way I spoke to people became more important than my grand plans of impressing the masses. After several months, it was confirmed that the tumor was benign. But the insights and lessons I learned were living and intense.

There is another strange dimension to this story. When I was a music composition student in college, I made up this crazy song, "I gotta purple stain all over my brain, purple stain." Who knows what made me say such meaningless words, but those were the lyrics that I sang repeatedly. Several years later I was lying on the MRI machine while a purple dye was injected into my vein in order to enable the doctors to see how it flowed through my brain. My song came true. I had a purple stain all over my brain. I guess we should be careful what we sing about.

There is really no reason we should be victims in order to learn the crucial lessons of life. Although the emotional impact of personal tragedy has a far greater effect than when we hear of it happening to someone else, logically it should make no difference. The trick is to develop this level of awareness while we are still safe and healthy. We can do this by developing our power of imagination. When we hear of some misfortune befalling someone—which, if you read the newspapers, you most likely encounter every day—you should spend a few moments contemplating what the event was like. What would you have felt had you been there? How would it change your life? Of course, the emotional impact of someone else's personal tragedy is much less than if it happens to us in our own lives. Most of the time, reports of other people's travails engender in us only brief moments of empathy, until the feelings and the memory of the sad story fade away. Even when tragedy strikes close to home, its impact is often temporary, unless we take some positive action to keep the message alive. Human beings are strangely resistant to the very thing that can bring them the most happiness.

Therefore, to inspire positive change not only requires a powerful wake-up call, it must be followed with some effort that turns the inspiration into a lasting lesson that is reflected in everyday action.

～ Setting Out on the Road

Let us remember that positive change can happen naturally by simply thinking deeper into those type of experiences that we are already drawn to that inspire a positive emotional impact. Sometimes these present us with a positive vision of our future, though at other times, we can sense something unhealthy about our idealized image. This too can serve as a powerful warning to slow down and re-evaluate our choices. At other times, it takes a tragedy close to home to jar us out of our complacency. But that too should be seen for the best.

A number of years ago, I was fortunate to serve as a host for one of my favorite jazz piano players of all time, Herbie Hancock. He was in Jerusalem for a concert and I spent the day with him. Starting in the Old City, I got to hear him play on my friend's piano. Then I took him to the Kotel and we got to shmooze about a number of issues. We eventually made our way to a music school in Jerusalem where he was invited to speak to a group of music students.

On the way, I asked him the following question, "If, God forbid, you were to lose your fingers, would you have what to live for?" He paused for a minute and said to me, "I have actually been thinking about that question for many years and I can finally say, Yes, I do have what to live for."

We continued to the music school where he answered a number a questions about chords and jazz harmony. Then he decided to tell the class about the question that I asked him on the way. The students looked quite shocked. Not only did their non-Jewish hero walk in with this religious guy, but he decided to quote me when shifting the topic away from the music and on the spiritual awareness that there is so much more to life than jazz. If we just think about what we know to be truly meaningful, it can save us many years of traveling down the wrong path.

Journal

1. What do you depend on the most to achieve your career, favorite hobby or creative talent?

2. If, God forbid, you lost use of that ability, would you be able to live a happy life?

3. If not, ask yourself why your happiness is dependent upon that skill.

Spiritual Gender

In our journey to discover who and what you are, it would be foolish to overlook the fact that God made you either male or female. This is not to create any stereotypes that place expectations on either gender. Rather, we would like to acknowledge that the fact that you were born male or female is another powerful hint to a part of your spiritual identity that can only be helpful in seeing the bigger picture of who you are.

Your gender plays an important part in some of the major choices you make in life. The way the physical reality of your body functions is a piece of the overall puzzle of how you were born and therefore your gender must be considered as an important part of the real you. So if you are an artsy, idealistic or brainy personality, you must also include that you are a male or female artsy, idealistic or brainy personality.

⟿ Physical Reflection of Spiritual

Why should your gender play any role in your individuality? Making such an assertion is almost heresy in the Western world today. As we have discussed, there is a basic mystical idea that everything in the physical world is a reflection of something in the higher spiritual world. If you were created male, you have something male to achieve in this world and if you were created female you are here to achieve something female. This does not limit you in any way. Rather, it frees you from having to waste your time looking in the wrong place—because you know that you were created to be who you really are.

ᴥ Masculine Energies / Feminine Energies

When looking deeper into the idea of being created in the image of God and the ten *sefiros*, we discover fascinating insights about the concepts of gender and relationships. Although we generally refer to God as "He," the truth is that there are many times when God is referred to in the feminine. That is because some of the attributes are male, some are female and some are both.

Let's re-examine some of the principles that taught us about the nature of the ten *sefiros* underlying creation. If you look closely at the diagram showing the *sefiros*, you will notice that all the *sefiros* in the right column have more to do with giving, expanding and taking initiative whereas the ones on the left bear the common theme of receiving, contracting, self-control and submissiveness. The Kabbalah considers these paradigms of masculine and feminine energies. As for the middle column, it represents the common theme of balance and integration and the deepest love between the male and female.

Furthermore, since the *sefiros* represent that pattern upon which all human beings are created in the Divine image, this also tells us more about what it means to have been created male or female and what our souls are truly striving toward in a loving relationship.

ᴥ We All Have Some of Both

It is important to keep in mind that since we are all created in the image of God, we must all have each of the ten attributes. That means that every male, although he may predominantly express male attributes, also has a left side, with a representation of female attributes as well. This is of course the same for women, who have predominantly female attributes, but also a right side with a taste of male attributes. This means that although it may seem like men are from Mars and women are from Venus, there is a little of Mars and Venus in all of us. Just as it helps a *Gevurah* personality understand a *Chessed* personality by finding some of that trait within himself, so a man who is struggling to understand his wife, can do so more easily by identifying the female attributes already within him.

～ The Gender of *Sefiros*

Let's try to look at the male and female attributes so as to understand some of the strengths and weaknesses that are an essential part of the "real you." Keep in mind that when discussing the gender of the *sefiros*, we are speaking of supernal archetypes, which do not always neatly fit specific men and women. Some men are born with or have developed more female spiritual attributes and some women are born with or have developed more male spiritual attributes. Even on a biological level, although male energy is primarily based on a man's level of testosterone, and woman's energy on her natural estrogen, both genders contain small amounts of the hormones found in the other. Similarly, on the spiritual level, we should not run our lives solely driven by the dominant attribute of our gender; rather, we should try to tap into our own supply of the opposite gender attribute. This is how we are able to create balance, and, in addition, understand our spouse better. When we unite and work together with our spouse, we are able to get to an even higher level of the opposite attribute, since they provide it more naturally.

～ Male and Female within the Ten *Sefiros*

As we explained, the *sefirah* of *keser* (crown) represents the contact point for the Endless Light to enter creation. Therefore, it contains both male and female energies within it in an undifferentiated way, before the genders become divided.

~ *Chochmah* **and** *Binah*

The first split into male and female *sefiros* comes with *chochmah* and *binah*. Thus, *chochmah*, which heads the right column, is sometimes called *Abba*, Father, and *binah*, which heads the left column, is sometimes referred to as *Imma*, Mother. *Chochmah* is the first of the "intellectual" *sefiros* and corresponds to the right side of the brain. It represents God's initial concept of creation; God's flash of vision to create a world, before all the details were worked out.

As we explained earlier, *chochmah*, in the consciousness, is a flash of intuitive insight, a moment in which an entire concept is grasped in its undifferentiated totality. In Hebrew, the letters of *chochmah* also spell out *koach mah*, meaning, the potential for whatever is. This is considered a male trait, because psychologically, men are more given over to spontaneous ideas than women; their creative minds run in such a way that makes it difficult for them to always actualize their vision. They can be involved with numerous projects at once, though find it difficult to complete any one of them. In terms of relationships, they often find it hard to commit and settle down, as they prefer the expansive state of raw potential, rather than the limited (though growth-producing) state of relationship. And on the biological level, all that a man brings to the creation of a child is a spark, a tiny point, a drop of potential. It is the woman who expands and builds upon it.

"Behind every great man is a great woman." It is this power of *binah*, to "flesh out" and develop the flash of *chochmah* that makes it a feminine trait. Another feature identified with the property of *binah* is the ability to explain and elucidate concepts both to oneself and others. The word *binah* is related to the word *boneh*, as we explained, and also the Hebrew root *bein*, which means "between," since it is the power of the feminine to draw connections *between* things—between ideas or between people.

Kabbalah regards the relationship between *chochmah* and *binah* to be a continual union. The *Zohar* calls them "two companions that never separate." It is through this union that the world continues to exist, and, in the individual, it is through this union that thoughts move from the realm of the abstract, to those which enter into the emotions to touch one's heart.

～ The Lower Seven—Emotions and Actions

Whereas the first triad of *sefiros*—*keser*, *chochmah* and *binah*—correspond to the intellectual attributes of a human being, the seven lower *sefiros* correspond to the emotional and physical aspects of a person and sit below the head within the human shape of the *sefiros*. These seven *sefiros* represent the lower yet more relatable world that we live in. The seven days of creation, the seven years of agricultural cycle, the role of our forefathers in building the world and other important spiritual foundations correspond to these seven *sefiros*. Created in God's image, we were designed to reflect these attributes. By understanding the supernal paradigms of masculine and feminine that they represent, we can better understand how we as men and women relate emotionally and physically to the world, to ourselves and to each other.

～ *Chessed* and *Gevurah*—Expansion and Contraction

As we saw earlier, the trait of *chessed* is expansive. It is associated with a person's desire to embrace all of creation and bestow love and goodness upon it. This expansive force and connection to its external surroundings is a clear expression of the masculine role of *chessed* within the *sefiros*.

On the other hand, we earlier saw how the *Gevurah* personality is associated in the soul with the power to restrain one's innate urge to bestow goodness upon others, when the recipient of that good is judged to be unworthy and liable to misuse it. As the force that measures and assesses the worthiness of creation, *gevurah* is also referred to in Kabbalah as *midas ha-din* (the attribute of strict judgment). It is the restraining might of *gevurah* which allows one to overcome his enemies, be they from without or from within (such as one's evil inclination).

The advantage of the male *chessed* attribute is in its creative excitement to produce new things with the trust in their potential. The advantage of *gevurah* is the ability to determine which ideas are realistic and which are likely to fail.

Being that Kabbalah regards *gevurah* as a feminine trait, this provides a very interesting insight. Traditional Western models of femininity tend to define women as weak and passive. Kabbalah, however, associates women with strength; particularly, the inner strength that allows them to create viable structures, such as in the home, but also, in business or in the world.

If we were to relate these concepts to male-female relationships, we could say that men are meant to be the more giving partner in the relationship, though also, by their very nature, their role in a relationship is more unstable. They have a harder time controlling their urges and committing themselves to the restrictions of home, marriage and family life. The animal soul of a man and that of a woman will act differently if not disciplined. If a man's *chessed* is not controlled his attribute of love and initiative can cause it to be very distracted from his true life. Man's animal soul will easily be drawn after what they see. The challenge for men to guard their eyes from looking at women and considering inappropriate thoughts is very challenging if they have not developed the proper self-control. The mind of a man can easily generate fantasies that spread to the heart and then potentially to action.

Women, on the other hand, are far more gifted at structure and continuity in a relationship. In general, their being rooted in *gevurah* makes them more willing to settle down and begin a family. (Although in today's secular world, this distinction is becoming less obvious due to social reasons.) However, this very proclivity for structure can become negative, and express itself in criticism and demands that a husband finds offensive. Often a woman's need to feel the stability and loyalty of her husband will lead her to creating a smothering sense of restriction that can cause the impulsive nature of her husband to feel threatened. This can produce the exact opposite from what she had intended.

We see a fascinating reflection of this idea in the biological relationship of a husband and wife. Reproductively, the male is the giver and the woman, the receiver. In fact, the man transmits so much potential life that it would be impossible for any single woman to actualize it all. The woman's role is to take only a single spark of potential life, and develop it into reality. The average woman can have up to twenty babies in a regular lifespan, while men potentially could have thousands.

⤳ How to Truly Give

In a marriage, it is very important to understand these differences in order to share a truly loving relationship. Knowing how we are different allows us to give selflessly to one another. Rather than giving what you want for yourself, you must learn what the other person wants. The world for love in Hebrew is *ahava*, which means to give. True love will be developed by giving what the other person really wants and needs, not by projecting your needs onto them.

> *Rebbe Nachman of Breslov asks: We know that preference is given to the right side over the left. When doing mitzvos or even getting dressed in the morning we try to use the right side first. Yet when God created us, He put the heart which is the most central organ on the left side. Why? The answer is that when a man and woman come together and face each other, the heart of the one they love is on their right. That is because true love is when you give according to what the receiver is in need of rather than based on what the giver feels like giving.*

The Freezer Story

I learned this lesson early in my marriage, when I bought my wife a romantic gift for our first anniversary. At the time we lived in an apartment in the Old City of Jerusalem with a tiny kitchen. We had many guests for Shabbos, but there was never enough room in the fridge to keep all the food my wife prepared. Thus, instead of preparing everything slowly, days in advance, my wife stayed up very late Thursday night preparing all the food, so that it wouldn't spoil before Shabbos without refrigeration.

So, being a naive youth, I decided that I would get the awesome gift of a little freezer to handle the extra food. So off I proudly went downtown, to buy my wife a romantic freezer. (By the way, if you are a man, you probably think I was right. If you are a woman, you are already laughing at me for my stupidity.)

Soon, I returned home with a cold freezer to melt my wife's heart. "Honey, look what I bought you." Well, it was obvious from the frozen look on her face that she had been expecting something else—a hot piece of jewelry, no doubt.

"Is there something wrong?" I asked.

"Well," she said, far too politely, "I appreciate what you got but I was hoping to get something more mushy."

"But I thought the point of a freezer is to keep things from getting mushy," I replied.

"No, I meant mushy like some diamond earrings and a mushy card."

That was many years ago, and since then, our relationship has changed. Now she wants the freezer with a mushy card. But the important lesson I had to learn was to give her what she wanted. Even though she needed the freezer, it was not a romantic gift.

~ *Netzach, Hod, Yesod*

When we look at the next triad of *sefiros*, we find *netzach* on the right thigh, *hod* on the left thigh and *yesod* on the reproductive organ. *Netzach* is a derivative of *chessed* in that an ongoing flow of *chessed*, located just above it, creates the overwhelming dominance of *netzach*. Similarly the flow of *gevurah* creates the restraint that allows for the empathy of *hod* to make room for another individual to express themselves. *Yesod* is achieved through the balance of *netzach* and *hod*. In a healthy relationship, both man and wife must provide direction and positive influence while leaving space for their spouse to be who they are without becoming lost.

God designed the world in a way for us to utilize the physical world to reach the greatest level of spiritual fulfillment. Through a deeper understanding of why we are created with physical drives, we can find powerful insight about how the male and female relationship is ultimately supposed to be expressed.

There are a number of places in the Torah where the relationship between God and the Jewish people is described as a loving relationship between a man and a woman. That is because there are so many spiritual, emotional and physical parallels that are given to us to enjoy; marriage serves as a means to elevate ourselves to a high spiritual level of fulfillment. As stated by R. Aryeh Kaplan, a married couple in love is a counterpart of the male and female archetypes on high. Therefore, when a husband and wife are intimate, they can completely identify themselves with the Divine as a gift of God and experience a deep sense of thankfulness. They can be aware of the spark of the Divine in the pleasure itself and elevate or conceal it. When they direct this power to righteousness and spiritual wholeness, they arouse an influx of Divine blessing into the world. When they pervert their mission, they cause the opposite.[52]

---

52. R. Aryeh Kaplan, *Inner Space*.

The ability for a man and wife to be able to create new life to-gether is the ultimate expression of being created in God's image. God used both male and female attributes to create man; through our own union of man and woman we can reunite the male and female attributes within us, and like a chain up to the *sefiros*, we can bring a new life into the world. It is because there is so much spiritual potential that people feel such a need for relationships and such a sense of loneliness and longing when they lack it. Be-ing aware of this essential spiritual part of the longing of our soul is critical in considering what the motives are behind emotional drives and distractions. Knowing what you are ultimately looking for in marriage and what is just illusion, can either save you from years of chasing things that are not what your soul is looking for, or from not appreciating the potential in your own marriage.

⁓ **Summary**

Since God decreed for you to be either male or female, you should take that fact very seriously when considering what you are looking for in life. If you are man, struggling with the male challenge of *chessed* urges, you can rest assured that you are not struggling in this alone. It is an integral part of being a man, and the Torah gives tools to address that challenge. It also comes with the reward of learning to discipline it. If you are a women frus-trated by behaviors of the world around you, it is important to know that it is a problem to find true and positive expressions of *gevurah*.

The Prophet Within

Congratulations. We are entering the deepest point in our journey. Standing on the border between tangible and abstract landscapes, we are about to take a look at that inner voice, that gut feeling that tells you to make a choice in your life. How do you know when to trust that voice? Is it what your soul is really calling out for, or is it just the "lie within the truth" doing its best to convince you to do something wrong? The soul is abstract and so must be the method of hearing what it is saying. But thank God we have the wisdom of the Torah to help us find our way home.

In ancient times, when prophets walked the earth, a unique and foolproof means of coming to know oneself was available. The prophets of ancient Israel were not merely teachers and guides who sought to elevate the people ethically, morally and spiritually. Nor were their prophecies merely concerning future events, such as wars, exiles or even the messianic times. A prophet was a person who had a direct connection to God. God spoke to him (or her) and through him (or her). In addition to the prophets whose words are recorded in the Tanach, there were literally millions of other prophets existing throughout the land of Israel during the period of the Judges and the First Temple — from roughly 1150 BCE to about 400 BCE. They helped people with their everyday problems and decisions, even the most mundane: where to live, what to invest in or how to find lost items. They voiced not simply their own opinions, but the word of God that spoke through them.

Thus, in those days, if you wanted to know about your true purpose in life, you could go to a prophet and ask him. With his prophetic vision, he would look deep into your soul, and tell you who you are. His words were God's words, his message was undeniable. And when you would hear it, you would know that it was true. It would cut through all the mental doubts and confusion that you might have.

What was it that they were seeing in the person? We are taught that when the prophet would find the true will of the person, what they were really sensing was the will of God being expressed through that individual and for that individual. This means that every person is created with a pure desire to do the will of God according to the individual mandate that has been designed specifically for them. There is a voice somewhere inside each and every one of us telling us who we are and what we are here to achieve. More amazingly, this inner voice is the meeting place between our truest sense of self, and God's own desire for us; in a word, our God-given mission.

Today, we no longer have prophets. Prophecy ended toward the beginning of the Second Temple period, around twenty-three centuries ago. But the Vilna Gaon explains that in our time every person still maintains a degree of *ruach haKodesh*, Divine inspiration, which enables them to become aware of their own, unique calling in life. If we are clear enough, we can actually realize our purpose, and God's will for us. However, if there is any self-interest or impure motives in our thinking, it will lead us away from fulfilling God's will.

In such a confusing world, with so many voices that influence us to cover up our pure motives, we need help to find our way back to hear the will of God through our true inner selves. Since, when true prophecy ceased, a remnant of prophetic wisdom remained with us from then until today, in essence, then, what we are seeking to uncover is not merely our deepest inclinations, but the spark of prophecy that was lost but remains hidden in the deepest recesses of our soul.

The key to understanding the process of excavating our deepest, most hidden treasures, lies in a simple verse from the book of Proverbs, written by King Solomon: "All of a person's ways seem right in his own eyes, for God is within the spirit."[53]

The Vilna Gaon (1720–1797) explains this concept. However, what he describes, as explained below, is a very advanced process. If the following ideas seem too out of reach or abstract at this point in your personal journey, you may skip the rest of this chapter. As we discussed previously, a human being is created in the image of God. Not in any physical way, since God transcends all physicality. According to Kabbalah, a human being resembles God through his thoughts and actions. Of course, God Himself totally transcends creation (thoughts and actions included). However, God reveals and manifests Himself through creation, similar to the way that the soul reveals itself through the thoughts and actions of the mind and body. The entirety of creation, from this physical world all the way to the highest, most pristine spiritual world, is the vehicle through which God manifests Himself in creation. Kabbalah speaks of four primary, spiritual worlds: *Atzilus*, *Beriyah*, *Yetzirah* and *Assiyah*. These are composed of endless gradations, which serve as filters, or vehicles, by means of which God runs the world.

These worlds, or spiritual dimensions, also exist in us. They are the vessels we use to express ourselves and move from potential, through thought to action. The four spiritual worlds also correspond to the first four levels of soul, which we discussed earlier. All of these, in turn, correspond to God's essential Name—the

---

53. Proverbs 16:2.

YHVH (the Tetragrammaton)—which expresses God's creative essence, as it filters down through the worlds.

⤳ What You Really Want

This single, universal pattern between the upper worlds and human beings means that a spiritual correspondence exists between them. Our thoughts, speech and actions are a microcosm of God's own creative energy, which flows constantly into creation. According to the Vilna Gaon, if a human being could sufficiently purify his body and soul, till the point that he is no longer drawn after lower cravings and desires, then he has removed the dirt that covers his soul, and can become a vehicle for the Divine Name, or the Divine Presence, which will manifest itself through him. At that moment, there is a correspondence.

In other words, if a person could totally purify himself, then the Divine Presence would rest upon him and move through him. This is the meaning of the verse above: "...for God is within the spirit." When a person is totally aligned with God's will—when God moves within his spirit—then everything he does, i.e., his will, his inclinations, his desires, goals and drives, are manifestations of God's will. At this point, a person has become "transparent," so that what God wants, he wants, and what God desires, he desires. Such a person would be a living manifestation of God's will in the world. Kabbalistically, this is what it means to become a *merkavah*, a "chariot," for the Divine Presence. Just as a rider directs a chariot where he wants, so God directs the person—through his own will and conscious choices—where God wants. If a person could purify himself enough, there would be a complete alignment between his own will and God's will for him and the world. Since God wants what is ultimately best for us, there is nothing more that we really want than to do His will.

But how does this relate to us, who are far from this level of purity and spiritual attachment? This is implied by the first part of the verse. "All of a person's ways seem right in his own eyes."[54] According to the Vilna Gaon, this refers to the first thought that arises in a person's mind, in any given situation: a thought—or perhaps better described as an "intuition"—that we always seem to favor in the long run over other, subsequent thoughts. We all have a natural inclination to be drawn after our first thought: the first impression of another person or the first impulse that arises in a new situation. The Vilna Gaon is saying that there is a level of true knowledge that arises in the senses, before thought enters into the complex system of doubts, self-centered desires and inclinations, which still reflects its source. A person's first thought about any topic or decision has the potential of being the purest thought, and the one that most reflects God's will for us in that instant. This is a taste of prophecy that remains with us, even after the prophets have ceased.

Practically speaking, this means that if you are looking for an answer to your deepest, most pressing question; if you want to know what God wants from you in this world, the way to discover it is two-fold:

First, you must clear away as much debris and junk as you can from your mind. You must find a quiet, undisturbed place and time when you can ask yourself your deepest questions, and honestly listen to yourself for an answer. R. Nachman of Breslov suggests going out into the country, away from the city noise and hustle, and even then, staying up until late at night, when the world is quiet. Then, when you think about your life, or when you pray to God, your words will be enriched with a power that is beyond your own.

Try to find a quiet place and ask yourself a question that relates to a life choice, and listen to the first answer that comes to your mind. Do you like the answer? Does it register with you? Does it sound true? If so, it may be your fate and God's will. Ask it

---

54. Proverbs 16:2.

again, worded differently, from a different direction. Stay attuned to your spontaneous feelings and impulses; don't yet judge. Did you get the same answer? If so, there is one more step you need, before you can truly rely upon it.

The next step is to take that initial, powerful thought, and examine it even closer, for we can only rely on it if it is *completely free* of even the slightest self-interest. The Vilna Gaon explains that if even the slightest trace of self-interest is present in this meditation, and not identified as such at the beginning, a person may rely upon his first impression—which is really self-induced—and follow it down the wrong path, until his life is completely ruined. That is a frightening idea, and illustrates just how much is at stake. This is why it is important to work on this process when you feel you have acquired a strong enough sense of yourself to be able to spot selfish motives influencing your thoughts.

⌒ Remove Yourself to Find Yourself

The trick, then, is to *take oneself out of the picture*. After you have asked yourself the million-dollar question and heard an answer that seems to arise spontaneously from your heart, you have to step back and very carefully sift through the response. Remove all self-interests, regard the situation objectively. Balance the enthusiasm and truth of your spontaneous answer with a cold and reflective rationality. The best way to do this is to look at yourself in the third person. If someone came to you for counsel, with a similar problem, and you knew them as well as you know yourself, would you give them this piece of advice? Would you tell them to move forward with their first impulse, or would you tell them to wait, to temper their impulse, or to drop it altogether in light of other factors.

Now tell this to yourself. Admittedly, this can be very hard. It demands absolute authenticity and truth, and it may entail dropping some of your most cherished self-illusions (or delusions). But if you can do this, and your initial answer still remains; if you can say, Yes, this is what I have to do, then you can know that your decision is God's own will for you. You have experienced a small taste of prophecy.

At that point, you reach the third stage where you can enjoy the clarity of knowing that you have objectively uncovered the best choice. Now you can move forward and live the choice with a full sense of conviction and passion free of the confusion and doubts that place a damper on the quality of life. Let it all go.

I wanna see you laughing
see the little signs of life that's on the way

And I wanna see you free at last
goodbye to the past
no more looking back
time to spread our wings and fly away

Let it all go
Let it all go now
Time to move beyond the lonely child

Let it all go
Let it all go now
Above the world that never likes to see you smile[55]

55. From my song, "Let it All Go."

Part III
Making It
REAL

Making Clear Choices

U nfortunately, many people can acquire tremendous insight into what is best for them yet still feel blocked by a fear of making decisions. This can be extremely frustrating for people who truly want to move forward but can't seem to face the challenge of choosing one option over the others. We are therefore going to discuss a few examples of such fears and some ways to help get past them.

∼ Fear of Failure

The inability to act on a good option is often a result of the fear of failure. Yet, we must remember that even the most brilliant minds make mistakes, most of which are unavoidable. As we will discuss, if you wait to have a hundred percent certainty about important decisions, you are unlikely to ever fulfill them. That is because most of life's most fateful decisions, such as career, major investments, marriage partner, home purchase and even religious affiliation, are made with a strong dose of uncertainty. By facing this reality, it makes it much easier to move forward with the best you can do within a reasonable amount of time to research the issue at hand. Even after thorough research, it's highly unlikely that a person will not make a mistake in at least one of life's big areas, and crashing later in life can lead to disillusionment and disappointment.

Many people make improper choices in life largely because they did not invest enough time and objective thinking into their original evaluation of their options. Much of their unhappiness and disappointment could have been avoided had they put the time and effort into carefully weighing the choice. Of course, it's hard to blame a person if he has never been introduced to the wisdom and techniques available for making better life choices. Many people have never considered the possibility that there is a way to develop clarity in this area, and they become lost in the jungle, unaware of a nearby path that leads them home.

In the earlier chapters of this book, you have been given insight into who you are and what types of things will bring you the greatest level of happiness. Together with the proper thinking tools, these become the building blocks in designing the correct choices to be made.

One helpful tool is to remember that almost no choices are irreversible. Even poorly made choices are usually better than no choice at all, for they teach us more about ourselves and what is truly important in our lives. As we discussed, sometimes these lessons are learned through hardship or suffering, which everyone would like to avoid. However, most people who have faced and overcome suffering in life—whether as a result of their own poor choices, or due to extenuating circumstances—will readily affirm that they benefited deeply from the experience, both in terms of self-knowledge and personal growth. According to Kabbalah, sometimes a person has to go through many reincarnations until they repair the damage that their bad choices have made. However, in the end, every individual will reach spiritual perfection, and their soul will shine even more for having gone through the difficult experience.

Let's look closer at the issue of uncertainty when making a decision. We must remind ourselves that there are many critical life choices that we must make without knowing a hundred percent which is the best option to choose. But just because we do not have a hundred percent proof of the best decision to make, it does not mean that we cannot act on ninety percent or even fifty-one percent of the information at our disposal. There are times when people are forced into difficult situations and they must make the best choice they can with the little information available to them.

For instance, imagine someone is diagnosed with a serious illness. One doctor prescribes a certain type of treatment and another doctor prescribes a different one. The patient cannot invest ten years in medical school in order to become an expert in the field of his illness. And even if he did, would that make him more qualified than the authorities that are giving him conflicting advice? So he spends as much time as he can researching what the world experts have to say and which one is more reliable, then he makes his decision and prays that it is correct.

That last point is very important. Fear of irrevocable failure exists only in a world in which we do not believe that there is a higher power guiding us to our ultimate good. If we recognize that to be the case, then even if the decision we made, based upon the information we had at hand, turned out to be a bad one, we have to have faith that in the end, it will work out for the best.

Life is too valuable to give up the gift of thinking just because we cannot see the future. The Torah view is that we must do our part with whatever resources we have available, and afterward, leave it in the hands of God.

Journal

1. Think now about a decision you must make. Not too big and not too small.

2. Think of your best options to choose from.

3. Now imagine the worst that could happen if you don't choose the ultimate best option.

4. Go through the same steps with a bigger choice.

_____

_____

_____

_____

_____

_____

_____

_____

_____

_____

_____

_____

_____

_____

_____

⟿ Fear of Missing Out? (FMOBIA)

Another block many people face when making decisions is fear that by choosing one thing, they are going to miss out on something else. No matter what stage of the journey we are at or how long the journey is, we must face the fact that there are always options that are available that we are not going to be able to experience. That is not because someone is trying to restrict us; it is the nature of any experience. You can't expect to spend endless time in every place you dream of visiting. Furthermore, being in one place inevitably means that you are not somewhere else at that same time. In a sense, you are always missing out on what is going on elsewhere. For some people, the fear of missing out on something is so haunting that they end up missing out on everything. They are living on the fence of every life choice—their career, relationships and even petty choices, such as what clothes to buy or what to do that evening.

To really enjoy every step of your life, it is important to choose what you really want to. Take the time to ask yourself what would make you happiest, what would benefit your future the most and how feasible these options are. Once you have done your best within the time you have available, you must put aside the calculative side of your mind and jump in to experience it to the fullest—a hundred percent commitment to get the most out of it, even though there are endless options that you did not choose.

Those who fear making choices should therefore be aware that not choosing is even scarier. The anxiety created by the feeling of missing out on something leads to the even bigger loss of not enjoying any choice you made. It's worth just doing the best you can, with the choices at your disposal, and trusting that in the end, you will come out ahead. Live your choice to the fullest and you will come out a winner.

Journal

1. Think about the last time you enjoyed yourself without being haunted by inner voices telling you that something else may be more exciting.

2. Compare that pleasure to another time when you were too preoccupied with your options and therefore could not enjoy yourself at all.

3. Use this comparison to make it easier to commit to one pure choice in the future.

_____

_____

_____

_____

_____

_____

_____

_____

_____

_____

_____

_____

_____

⌐ Procrastination

Another powerful tool to help us make the best choices is to remind ourselves of our mortality in this world. One of the consequences of Adam having eaten from the Tree of Knowledge was that from that point on, man was going to face the new reality of death. This reality can be seen as a gift, for without awareness of our limited time in the world, we would unlikely feel motivated to savor our time and make careful decisions about what is truly most important to us.

We must remind ourselves not to slide into the habits of life without leaving room to reevaluate our priorities and to make sure we are on the best path toward their fulfillment. I can't imagine anything more frustrating than to look back at my life with regret for all the choices I could have made if I had only taken some time out to prioritize.

Journal

1. What are the most important goals you would like to accomplish in your life?

2. By what age do you hope to achieve them?

3. What must you do now in order to reach these goals by then?

Quick Review

The goal of this chapter is to try to keep alive all the messages of this book. Here is a brief review of the main points followed by a list of questions to help keep the ideas fresh. Even if you don't read the book again, I highly recommend reviewing the questions to help keep your life vision and spiritual clarity in focus as much as possible.

First, you must never forget the answer to "Who are you?" By zooming in on the uniqueness of your personality, you create the awareness of what is needed to satisfy those traits and preferences. Considering the three main personalities, which one did you identify with the most? Was there another personality that you felt was also identifiable, yet not enough to be your primary one? Is the third, least relatable personality something that you struggle with in your life?

By putting the pieces together, you must consider providing yourself with a strong dose of what naturally invigorates you together with a program to help face the weaknesses that hold you back from fulfilling your potential. Some people tend to focus only on their strengths. For example, if they are a *Gevurah* personality, they may be busy from morning to evening accomplishing numerous tasks in an organized and effective way. But if they don't stop to breathe the air, think about the bigger picture of life and connect to people in a healthy emotional way, they will miss out on so much of what life has to offer. By complimenting your natural skills with a program to develop your area of weakness, you will not only become more well-rounded, but you will improve the quality of your natural skills as well.

Second, never forget the answer to the question "What are you?" The more you drive home the message that you are an elevated being, divinely created with a priceless jewel inside, the more you will ensure that you will live a life of meaning. As the world works so hard to make us forget our intrinsic value as a human soul, we must make an ongoing effort to internalize this awareness even though it is something we claim to know. We need to teach our hearts the lesson of "what are you" so it affects the way we act, not just the way we think.

∾ Outside Influences

The path of our journey has been inward, but in our daily lives—unless we are living in the ideal spiritual environment—we expose our souls to all kinds of external factors that have a profound effect on us. Abraham was told to "go to himself," which started by leaving his negative environment in order to hear his own inner voice. Only later was he directed to a positive environment. But not all of us have the luxury to choose to live where our souls will benefit from the clean air and pure surroundings. Can we avoid the pollution that fights against our mindfulness, inner peace and other factors of spiritual awareness? The answer is yes—by working to improve your existing environment.

When you have the option as to who to spend time with, try to consider what they are likely going to pull you toward. Your friends are often the ones who shape how you spend your spare time, and if they are only interested in things that are counterproductive, you are going to have a hard time staying away from these. You can be making tremendous progress on your journey, working to build your inner awareness and ability to live up to higher standards, but within a brief animated phone call from a friend, easily lose much of the benefits and drift off on a path that could lead into polluted waters.

If you want to continue growing, create an environment where it is conducive to do so. Do you want to continue learning more about yourself and what the Torah has to offer you? Place yourself among others who are doing the same. Find a rabbi, teacher, a mentor or a group of people dedicated to growing. Being in a learning environment is, in itself, a great nourishment for the soul.

Journal

1. Who do you know that will have a positive effect on you if you are around them more?

2. Think about who may be having a negative effect on you and try to minimize their influence.

Review Where You Want to Get to

Okay, here is the list of questions based on many of the topics discussed on our journey.

1. Make a list of some of the main goals and values that your society is telling you to live up to.

2. What do you agree with?

3. What do you disagree with?

4. What do you think is your main personality type?

5. What do you think is your secondary personality type?

6. Which personality type do you find most difficult to get along with?

7. Try to look at your life like a stranger. Look at your home, possessions and the personality it all portrays. Ask yourself, Who is this? Try to keep this impression as part of your image of who you are.

8. Try to identify one of your positive attributes that you would like to build upon. It must be natural and invigorating to you.

9. Identify one negative trait that you would like to work to improve upon.

10. What do you feel you have to offer your community or to the world as a whole?

11. Do you feel that you are in touch with your soul?

12. What distractions are interfering with your feeling of self-awareness?

13. Do you have a strong sense of self-esteem?

14. What can you tell yourself at times when you feel bad about yourself?

15. Review the concept of being created in the image of God. Try to create a short phrase to remind yourself of your intrinsic value as a soul.

16. Take a few minutes to identify experientially with each of the five levels of your soul.

17. What types of events have woken you up to the deeper meaning of life?

18. Try to increase this awareness without the need for anything dramatic having to happen in your life.

19. Being aware of your "spiritual gender" should help you know how to build your marriage or understand what you are looking for in a spouse. Is that true for you?

20. Give yourself space to dig deep beneath the surface of your identity and try to hear what your inner voice is saying. This can only be done when you have worked hard to remove the ego and extraneous thoughts and feelings from interfering with the purity and sincerity of the inner voice.

ᴄ **A Goodbye Note**

Although we have arrived at the end of this book, in no way has our journey come to a close. I hope you will continue to travel to higher levels of soul awareness and fulfillment of your individual purpose throughout the rest of your life. Feel free to keep in touch with me via my contact information below and my music which was written to complement the message of this book.

Thank you for reading,
David

> *Kabbalistic journey to the other side of your mind*
> *Discover the unique design*
> *See the wonders of your body and your soul*
> *The science you were never told*
> *The secrets of creation*
> *An inner revelation*
> *You are the destination*
> *Journey to the real you*[56]

david@realyouproject.com
www.realyouproject.com

---

56. From my song, "Journey to the Real You."

Personality Quiz

Choose which one describes you the most.

	A		B		C	
Based on this book, what primary personality type do you think describes you the best?	*Chessed*	☐	*Gevurah*	☐	*Tiferes*	☐
What interests you more?	Science	☐	Sports	☐	Art/Music	☐
What interests you more?	Halachah/ Jewish law	☐	Philosophy	☐	Mysticism	☐
What career would be most satisfying in terms of its day-to-day activity?	Business Management	☐	Medicine	☐	Sales	☐
Where are you most likely to be on holiday?	Mountain climbing	☐	Hanging out with people	☐	Visiting museums	☐
When you meet friends, when are you likely to show up?	On time	☐	A little late	☐	Very late	☐
Have you ever considered being a vegetarian?	I am one	☐	Yes, but not seriously	☐	Never	☐

Quiz add-up sheet

Skip to the next page when doing the quiz.
Check the same column that you checked for your answers to the quiz on the previous page.

A		B		C		POINTS
Chessed	⬭	*Gevurah*	⬭	*Tiferes*	⬭	3
Tiferes	⬭	*Gevurah*	⬭	*Chessed*	⬭	2
Gevurah	⬭	*Tiferes*	⬭	*Chessed*	⬭	2
Gevurah	⬭	*Tiferes*	⬭	*Chessed*	⬭	2
Gevurah	⬭	*Chessed*	⬭	*Tiferes*	⬭	1
Gevurah	⬭	*Tiferes*	⬭	*Chessed*	⬭	2
Chessed	⬭	*Tiferes*	⬭	*Gevurah*	⬭	1

Personality Quiz continued

	A		B		C	
How neat is your personal space such as your office or bedroom?	Total mess	○	Always neat	○	Depends on how busy I am with a project	○
What do you enjoy more?	Being alone, reading or developing an interesting project	○	It doesn't matter as long as I am doing something productive	○	Being among friends	○
Do you have a hard time saying no?	Usually	○	Sometimes	○	No	○
Do you find yourself busy every minute of the day?	Yes	○	No	○	I make a strong effort not to be	○
Are you bothered when people are late or messy?	Yes	○	No	○	Not if I see a reason why	○
Are you bothered when people are caught up in details?	Yes	○	No	○	A little	○
Do you tend to have long philosophical discussions with people?	Yes	○	No	○	Sometimes	○
What kind of entertainment do you enjoy the most?	Concert by your favorite musician	○	Circus with acrobats and special effects	○	Movie about the newest technology	○
What do you tend to focus on more?	Doing the right thing and getting the job done	○	People's feelings	○	Understanding the reasons behind something	○
How much do you tend to experience the moment?	Very little	○	Very much	○	Sometimes, when it is interesting to me	○

Quiz add-up sheet continued

Skip to the next page when doing the quiz.

A		B		C		POINTS
Chessed	☐	*Gevurah*	☐	*Tiferes*	☐	2
Tiferes	☐	*Gevurah*	☐	*Chessed*	☐	2
Chessed	☐	*Tiferes*	☐	*Gevurah*	☐	2
Gevurah	☐	*Chessed*	☐	*Tiferes*	☐	2
Gevurah	☐	*Chessed*	☐	*Tiferes*	☐	1
Chessed	☐	*Gevurah*	☐	*Tiferes*	☐	1
Tiferes	☐	*Gevurah*	☐	*Chessed*	☐	2
Chessed	☐	*Gevurah*	☐	*Tiferes*	☐	1
Gevurah	☐	*Chessed*	☐	*Tiferes*	☐	2
Gevurah	☐	*Chessed*	☐	*Tiferes*	☐	2

Personality Quiz continued

	A		B		C	
Are you the type to take care of details such as travel safety, scheduling and packing all the right things?	Yes	◯	No	◯	Medium	◯
How often do you stop to enjoy a beautiful sunset or scenery?	Whenever possible	◯	Very rarely	◯	Only if it looks exceptional	◯
What do you usually think when someone tries to convince you of a new theory about something?	Wow, that's really interesting	◯	Leave me alone, I don't have time for your theories	◯	I am going to prove them wrong as soon as I can get a word in	◯
Where are you most likely to be found very early in the morning?	At the gym or already on the way to my next activity	◯	Sleeping	◯	Getting up	◯
If something breaks the frame of your glasses, what are you most likely to do?	Get it fixed as soon as possible	◯	Find something to use to make it work, like a pin or tape or other makeshift solution	◯	Leave it until someone tells me that I should take care of it	◯
How do you feel when someone you don't know so well gives you a big hug?	Love it	◯	Hate it	◯	Bothers me because it's not sincere	◯
Do you have a good sense of direction?	Yes	◯	No	◯	Medium	◯
How do you deal with risk?	Very carefully	◯	Easygoing	◯	Depends on the level of risk	◯

Quiz add-up sheet continued

Skip to the next page when doing the quiz.

A		B		C		POINTS
Gevurah	☐	Chessed	☐	Tiferes	☐	2
Chessed	☐	Gevurah	☐	Tiferes	☐	1
Chessed	☐	Gevurah	☐	Tiferes	☐	1
Gevurah	☐	Chessed	☐	Tiferes	☐	2
Gevurah	☐	Tiferes	☐	Chessed	☐	2
Chessed	☐	Gevurah	☐	Tiferes	☐	3
Tiferes	☐	Chessed	☐	Gevurah	☐	1
Gevurah	☐	Chessed	☐	Tiferes	☐	1

Personality Quiz continued

	A		B		C	
What matches your character the most?	Waterfall	◯	Candle	◯	Raindrop	◯
Are you good at keeping a diet, exercise program or other change in lifestyle commitments?	Yes	◯	No	◯	Medium	◯
Are you good at making decisions?	Yes	◯	No	◯	Medium	◯
Do you like animals?	Yes	◯	No	◯	Medium	◯
Do you like to read?	Yes	◯	A little	◯	Only when it provides me with the tools to get something done	◯
Are you excited by new projects or events that your friends tell you about?	Usually	◯	Rarely	◯	Sometimes	◯
Are you good at completing projects?	Yes	◯	No	◯	Only when I really put my mind to it	◯
What most describes you?	Feeler	◯	Doer	◯	Analyzer	◯

Quiz add-up sheet continued

A		B		C		POINTS
Gevurah	☐	Chessed	☐	Tiferes	☐	1
Gevurah	☐	Chessed	☐	Tiferes	☐	1
Tiferes	☐	Chessed	☐	Gevurah	☐	1
Chessed	☐	Gevurah	☐	Tiferes	☐	1
Tiferes	☐	Chessed	☐	Gevurah	☐	1
Chessed	☐	Tiferes	☐	Gevurah	☐	1
Gevurah	☐	Chessed	☐	Tiferes	☐	1
Chessed	☐	Gevurah	☐	Tiferes	☐	2
Total =		Total =		Total =		

Add up the total Chessed, Gevurah and Tiferes answers. Note that some answers are worth more points than others, as marked in the far right column.

The highest points indicate your primary personality. Second highest points indicate your secondary personality.

About Mosaica Press

About Mosaica Press

Mosaica Press is an independent publisher of Jewish books.
Our authors include some of the most profound,
interesting, and entertaining thinkers and writers
in the Jewish community today.

There is a great demand for high-quality Jewish works
dealing with issues of the day — and Mosaica Press
is helping fill that need.

Our books are available around the world.
Please visit us at www.mosaicapress.com or
contact us at info@mosaicapress.com.
We will be glad to hear from you.

MOSAICA PRESS